THE WRITINGS OF JAMES STEPHENS

By the same author

THE DREAM PHYSICIAN, by Edward Martyn (*editor*)
EDUCATION FOR THE ITINERANT STUDENT

JAMES STEPHENS
Photograph by courtesy of Mrs Iris Wise

THE WRITINGS OF JAMES STEPHENS

Variations on a Theme of Love

Patricia McFate

First published 1979 by
THE MACMILLAN PRESS LTD
London and Basingstoke
Associated companies in Delhi
Dublin Hong Kong Johannesburg Lagos
Melbourne New York Singapore Tokyo

Typeset in Great Britain by
SANTYPE LTD, SALISBURY
and printed and bound in Great Britain
by W & J Mackay Limited, Chatham

British Library Cataloguing in Publication Data

McFate, Patricia
  The writings of James Stephens
  1. Stephens, James, b. 1882—Criticism
  and interpretation
  I. Title
  821′.9′12   PR6037.T4Z

  ISBN 0-333-24699-3

For Mary Bliss McFate
and Warren Cheston

Contents

Acknowledgements

Many people have contributed to this book, but none so
much as Iris and Norman Wise. Their kindness and help
have been a constant encouragement. Indeed, the book would
not have been possible without the aid of Iris Wise; she
has been most generous with her time and her information.
Professor Richard Finneran has also been obliging to me
in many ways. It was through his good offices that I first
met Mr. and Mrs. Wise, and I wish to thank him particularly
for that courtesy. His edition of the Stephens *Letters* has
been consulted frequently in the writing of the book; and
his chronology is one of the sources for the one which appears
in this volume.

The initial research for this book has been aided immeasur-
ably by Dr. Lola Szladits, Curator, the Henry W. and Albert
A. Berg Collection of the New York Public Library. Professor
Daniel Murphy has offered invaluable assistance with my
research in Ireland. Professor Richard Ellmann has served
as mentor, critic of my work, and good friend for many
years.

Others who, in the past and present, have given freely
of their time and to whom I am indebted include M. L.
Rosenthal, Liam Miller, Maurice Harmon, William Feeney,
Donald Torchiana, the late John Gordan, Vivian Mercier,
Janet Fendrych, Mrs. Thomas Bodkin, Mervyn Wall, Marjorie
Wynn, Michael Hanlon, Kenneth Goldstein, James McNulty,

and David Parson. My indebtedness to Sarkes Tarzian is beyond recompense.

For her participation in the bibliographical aspects of the study, I owe a debt of gratitude to Doretta Fuhs. I wish to thank Pam Gennusa, Loretta Dentley, and Miriam Boykin for cheerfully typing the many drafts of these chapters.

The research support provided by the Office of the Chancellor and the Graduate College of the University of Illinois at Chicago Circle and the staff support in the Office of the Vice Provost of the University of Pennsylvania are gratefully acknowledged. The Staffs of the Berg Collection, the National Library of Ireland, Newberry Library of Chicago, Northwestern University Library, and the British Museum have been consistently helpful.

The people to whom this book is dedicated provided the patience and understanding necessary to a writer. My mother and father encouraged me to begin my first studies of James Stephens fifteen years ago. Since that time, my mother and her family have given me more love and attention than I deserve. Warren Cheston is, in a real sense, responsible for the best parts of this book.

For permission to quote from the printed works and manuscripts of James Stephens, I am indebted to Mrs. Iris Wise; the Society of Authors, London; and the Henry W. and Albert A. Berg Collection, the New York Public Library, Astor, Lenox and Tilden Foundations. Quotations from *Letters of James Stephens* are reprinted by permission of Macmillan, London and Basingstoke. "And It Was Windy Weather" is reprinted with the permission of Macmillan Publishing Company, Inc., New York.

Chronology

1880	(9 February). Possible date of birth of James Stephens in Dublin.
1882	(2 February). Date of birth used by Stephens.
1886–96	Attended Meath Protestant Industrial School for Boys.
1896	Employed as a clerk by a Dublin solicitor, Mr. Wallace.
1901	On a gymnastic team which won the Irish Shield. Employed by Reddington & Sainsbury, solicitors.
1906	Employed as a clerk-typist in the office of T. T. Mecredy & Son, solicitors.
1907	Began regular contributions to *Sinn Féin*. Birth of stepdaughter, Iris, on 14 June; shortly thereafter announced that he had a wife, "Cynthia" (Millicent Josephine Gardiner Kavanagh, 22 May 1882–18 December 1960). Discovered by George W. Russell (AE).
1909	Acted in the Theatre of Ireland's two productions of Seumas O'Kelly's *The Shuiler's Child*. Birth of son, James Naoise, on 26 October. *Insurrections*.
1910	Acted in the Theatre of Ireland production of Gerald Macnamara's *The Spurious Sovereign*. Associated with David Houston, Thomas MacDonagh, and Padraic Colum in founding and editing the *Irish Review* (published March 1911–November 1914).

1911   Acted in Padraic O Conaire's *Bairbre Ruadh*. *The Marriage of Julia Elizabeth* produced by the Theatre of Ireland.

1912   *The Charwoman's Daughter; The Hill of Vision; The Crock of Gold.*

1913   Received a commission from *The Nation* (London) to write a series of short stories. Moved to Paris. Another production of *The Marriage of Julia Elizabeth* at the Hardwicke Street Theatre. *The Crock of Gold* awarded the Polignac Prize. *Here Are Ladies; Five New Poems.*

1914   *The Demi-Gods.*

1915   Elected Unestablished Registrar of the National Gallery of Ireland. *Songs from the Clay; The Adventures of Seumas Beg/The Rocky Road to Dublin.*

1916   *Green Branches; The Insurrection in Dublin.*

1918–24   Appointed Registrar of the National Gallery of Ireland.

1918   *Reincarnations.*

1919   Married "Cynthia" (then a widow) in London on 14 May.

1920   *The Wooing of Julia Elizabeth* (identical with *The Marriage of Julia Elizabeth*) produced at the Abbey Theatre by the Dublin Drama League. One of a series of operations for gastric ulcers. *Irish Fairy Tales.*

1922   *Arthur Griffith: Journalist and Statesman.*

1923   *Deirdre.*

1924   *Deirdre* presented the medal for fiction at the *Aonach Tailteann* festival. Resigned from the National Gallery (effective 1925). *Little Things; In the Land of Youth.*

1925   On lecture tour in America. Returned to London; shortly thereafter settled in the Kingsbury suburb of London. To America for another lecture tour. *A Poetry Recital; Christmas in Freelands.*

1926   *Collected Poems.*

1927   Friendship with James Joyce commenced. Joyce suggested that Stephens complete *Finnegans Wake* if he was unable to do so; this proposal made more formally in 1929.

1928   First BBC broadcast. Lecturer at the Third International Book Fair in Florence. *Etched in Moonlight; On Prose and Verse.*

1929   In Rumania; met Queen Marie. Trip to America; stay with W. T. H. Howe. *Julia Elizabeth: A Comedy in One Act; The Optimist; The Outcast.*

1930   Trip to America; stay with Howe. *Theme and Variations.*

1931   Trip to America; stay with Howe. *How St. Patrick Saves the Irish; Strict Joy.*

1932   Trip to America; stay with Howe. A founder member of the Irish Academy of Letters.

1933–35 Yearly lecture tours to America; visits with Howe.

1937   Began regular series of BBC broadcasts. Accidental death of son, James Naoise, on 24 December.

1938   *Kings and the Moon.*

1940   Moved to Woodside Chapel in Gloucestershire.

1942   Awarded British Civil List Pension.

1945   Returned to London.

1947   Awarded honorary D. Litt. degree from Dublin University (Trinity College).

1950   Final BBC broadcast. Death at Eversleigh on 26 December.

1 Stephens: the Man, the Writer, the Enigma

James Stephens was in many ways the most engaging of the modern Irish writers. He was witty and sympathetic, a brilliant conversationalist, and a fascinating story-teller. Many of those who have written about him in the past have emphasized his tiny stature and elf-like appearance, conferring on him titles such as the "Leprechaun of Irish Literature." This was not a totally unreasonable approach. Stories abound in which Stephens himself emphasized his physical imperfections; he often approached the world jokingly or ruefully displaying his wounds. Although he encouraged his identification with Seumas Beg (Little James), an anecdotal or impressionistic approach to his work is not adequate; Stephens is an artist deserving of precise study.

A contributor to the Irish Literary Revival, Stephens was friendly with William Butler Yeats, James Joyce, George Russell (AE), and George Moore, all of whom valued his wit and literary skill. With Yeats and AE, he was a student of Theosophical doctrine. Like Joyce and Moore he was interested in a realistic depiction of Ireland: his first novel, *The Charwoman's Daughter*, was a look at city life which preceded Joyce's *Dubliners* by four years. Following in the tradition of Yeats, Synge, AE, and Lady Gregory, Stephens produced an adaptation of the legends surrounding Deirdre (the Irish Iseult); he received the Tailteann Festival medal in 1924 for his novel *Deirdre*. In 1929 when Joyce wrote Harriet

Weaver that he planned to ask Stephens to complete the writing of *Finnegans Wake* if he became physically unable to finish the book, he reported that he was reading *Deirdre*. It is particularly interesting to study Stephens, then, because he shared interests with Joyce, Yeats, Synge, and others, and because his works, different as they are from theirs, are filled with a gaiety, a verbal complexity, and a richness of imagery not to be found in any other Irish writer of his period.

While Stephens' work has been the subject of scholarly investigation for some time, elements of his biography are still undergoing modification and questioning.

> "All books should be anonymous," said Mr. Stephens. "They ought to be published by a State Department, and should be known only by numbers."
> "Oh!" I expostulated.
> "Precisely," he uttered. "A book," he continued warmly, "is only to a limited extent the work of its titular author. It is really a communal effort, and, as such, it should be credited to the community it derives from."[1]

This dialogue, written by Stephens himself, sets forth the limitations and challenges he put upon a biographer. Although events in his vocational life are known — dates of publication of writings, various employments as clerk, registrar, and radio broadcaster — his personal life is difficult to trace.

His first critics accepted his statement that he, like James Joyce, was born on 2 February 1882.[2] One source even reported that Stephens and Joyce were born in the same hour, apparently taking to heart another remark made by Stephens.[3] In 1965 Hilary Pyle presented her evidence which agreed with what Oliver St. John Gogarty had first suggested in the *Dictionary of National Biography* — that Stephens was the child born on 9 February 1880 to Francis Stephens, a vanman, and his wife Charlotte Collins.[4] The matter remains unsettled, however, because Stephens' wife Cynthia claimed that this date was a guess, not a fact.

Richard Finneran has suggested three possibilities concerning Stephens' birth date: that Stephens was born "most likely illegitimate" at a time and place which he did not know;

that the date of 9 February 1880 is correct; that the date of 2 February 1882 is correct.[5] Finneran concludes that there is not enough evidence to make "a firm choice" among the alternatives. This is certainly true, although it is also true that there is at least one other possibility: that Stephens knew the correct birth date but wished to obscure it because his mother had remarried and he found himself unwanted or uncomfortable at home. If this were true, he might have changed his name in order to disappear from his family. The only known fact is that Stephens told his wife and his children that his birthday was on 2 February long before his friendship with Joyce, and he hinted to them that he had a stepfather with whom he disagreed.

Another legend, that Stephens grew up uneducated in the slums, has been questioned. According to Hilary Pyle, he was committed at the age of six to Meath Protestant Industrial School for Boys, a home for indigent or homeless children, and for ten years he lived at the school and attended its classes. Whether or not this is correct, it is known that in 1896 Stephens served as a junior clerk in the office of a solicitor by the name of Wallace. For the next sixteen years, he held the post of clerk-typist in several solicitors' offices, including those of Reddington and Sainsbury and Messrs. Mecredy.

During the period from 1896 to 1912, he was also engaged in a variety of activities outside of his employment. He was a member of the Dawson Street Gymnastic Club when it won the Irish Shield in 1901. As a fledgling writer, he sent his first contributions to Arthur Griffith in envelopes without return addresses, but by 1907 he was acquainted with Griffith, and his poems, essays, and short stories were appearing in *Sinn Féin* and *Sinn Féin Daily*, the newspapers which Griffith published. During the period between 1907 and 1911, over eighty items were printed by Griffith.

In 1907 Stephens also met his friend and mentor, AE (George Russell). The details of this meeting were recorded by George Moore in his book, *Vale*:

And every Thursday evening the columns of *Sinn Féin* were searched, and every lilt considered, and every accent noted; but the days and the weeks went by without a new "peep-o-peep, sweet, sweet," until the day that James Stephens began to trill; and recognizing at once a strange songster, AE put on his hat and went away with his cage, discovering him in a lawyer's office. A great head and two soft brown eyes looked at him over a typewriter, and an alert and intelligent voice asked him whom he wanted to see. AE said that he was looking for James Stephens, a poet, and the typist answered: "I am he."[6]

Under AE's direction he studied Theosophical literature and entered the literary world of Dublin.

Under Griffith's influence he attended Gaelic League classes and Sinn Féin political meetings. As early as 1905, Stephens was making notes for three lectures which he gave before the Gaelic Leaguers: the first was on the subject of Oliver Cromwell, Charles II, James II, and the Battle of the Boyne; another, on Douglas Hyde, "the greatest man in Ireland today"; and a third, on a return to the Irish language and customs. He also spent time at the Sinn Féin Club, which he praised in *Arthur Griffith* as a place which set an example of proper Irish behavior, provided education in a number of cultural areas, and developed "a spirit of friendship and the quality of self-reliance."

In 1907 Stephens was living as a lodger in the home of Millicent Gardiner Kavanagh and her husband, a doorkeeper or commissionaire at the Tivoli Theatre, a Dublin music hall. When the Kavanaghs separated shortly after the birth of their child, Iris, on 14 June of that year, Mrs. Kavanagh found lodging elsewhere, and presently Stephens joined her. Although they were not able to marry, Stephens informed his friends that Millicent (whom he called "Cynthia") was his wife, and he assumed the role of father to Cynthia's child. His and Cynthia's son, James Naoise, was born in 1909.

During this period his first book, *Insurrections* (1909), was published and his play, *The Marriage of Julia Elizabeth*, was performed in 1911 by the Theatre of Ireland, a company with which he occasionally acted. Between 1908 and 1911 six broadsides of poems and a serial of his first novel appeared;[7] the latter was printed in the *Irish Review*, a new journal which Stephens helped to edit.

When his first two novels, *The Charwoman's Daughter* and *The Crock of Gold*, and his second book of poems, *The Hill of Vision*, were published in 1912, their success — and the royalties he received from them — encouraged him to give up his career as a clerk and try to make a living as a writer. Seeking a greater knowledge of the world, Stephens and his family moved to Paris in May 1913. In November of that year, he was awarded the Polignac Prize for *The Crock of Gold*. When W. B. Yeats spoke to the Royal Society of Literature on the occasion of this award, he praised Stephens as a writer of promise and the novel as "a proof" that Dublin had "begun to live with deeper life."

With the exception of a short trip to Dublin in the late summer of 1914, Stephens and his family remained in Paris until August 1915. During his first year in Paris, he completed and published *Five New Poems* and *Here Are Ladies*, a collection of short stories. His third novel, *The Demi-Gods*, written in a Montparnasse cafe, Closerie des Lilas, was published in 1914. A charming story told about the writing of the novel goes that Stephens lost his manuscript while writing *The Demi-Gods* at the cafe. The waiter who found the tablet refused to accept a tip from its grateful owner because he too was a writer.

The Demi-Gods was followed in 1915 by two volumes of poetry, *Songs From the Clay* and *The Adventures of Seumas Beg*. Despite these accomplishments, and despite their love of Paris — Stephens maintained a flat in the city throughout his life — Cynthia and he were uneasy in Paris: the war depressed them and drained their energies, and Stephens discovered that it was impossible for him to write in that "sad," "dull" city. They left Paris in August 1915.

Not having secured enough financial success with his books to support his family, Stephens accepted a post as Registrar of the National Gallery of Ireland, a position he held for ten years. It was a joyful return to old friends and interests, and once more the "three great talkers in Dublin," Stephens, Stephen MacKenna, and AE, were united.[8] Stephens again studied Irish at Gaelic League classes and renewed an early interest in Old Irish literature.

His studies, his friendship with the scholars Edmund Curtis, Osborn Bergin, Richard Best, and MacKenna, and his readings

in the Irish Texts Society editions provided him with the
background for *Reincarnations* (1918), a collection of poems
adapted from the writings of several Gaelic poets. Stephens
utilized material from the most famous Irish saga cycles in
his next three books, which he later listed as his best works.
Irish Fairy Tales (1920) contained versions of stories from
the Fenian, mythological, and historical cycles.[9] In *Deirdre*
(1923) and *In the Land of Youth* (1924), he dealt with the
events in the Red Branch cycle leading to the Ulster-Connacht
war.[10] It had been Stephens' intention to present the remaining
tales in the Ulster cycle in three additional novels. Although
he finished a sixteen-chapter scenario, he never completed
this project.

The period between 1915 and 1925 included other works
beside those based on Old Irish material. Stephens was on
his way back to the National Gallery after lunch on Easter
Monday 1916 when he saw a barricade and witnessed a
shooting. Stephens had met one of the leaders of the Easter
Rebellion, Thomas MacDonagh, in 1910. A writer as well
as a patriot, MacDonagh had exchanged poems with Stephens,
worked with him as an editor of the *Irish Review*, and quarreled
with him briefly on political matters. But their friendship
continued until MacDonagh was executed in the aftermath
of the Uprising. Although Stephens disagreed with the radical
politics of the other leaders of the Rebellion, he wrote in
his preface to the *Poetical Works of Thomas MacDonagh* that
MacDonagh was a good man with a "longing for the hermit's
existence and a gift for gregarious life."[11] The Easter Rebellion
inspired a prose account, *The Insurrection in Dublin* (1916),
and an elegy, *Green Branches* (1916). Stephens also published
"Hunger" (1918), a short story which later appeared in
Etched in Moonlight; Arthur Griffith (1922), a tribute to his
deceased friend; and *Little Things* (1924), a volume of poetry.

In London in May 1919, he married Cynthia, whose first
husband had died. His sense of responsibility extended beyond
this ceremony to worry over the family income. His position
as Registrar, although not a demanding job (it was a generally-
acknowledged sinecure given to an artist so that he might
have time to do his work), did not pay a salary high enough
to cover expenses in Dublin. The Civil War had disturbed
Cynthia Stephens sufficiently to send the children to school

in England; a more private political scrimmage within the
departments of the National Gallery had wearied Stephens;
and his American friends and patrons, W. T. H. Howe and
Cornelius Sullivan, had encouraged him to come to the United
States for a lecture tour. In 1925 he resigned his post and
moved to London, where he and his family settled in a house,
"Eversleigh," in the Kingsbury suburb of London. This decision
was almost routinely condemned by his friends in Ireland
who believed that his removal from the scene of his literary
productivity was unwise. AE, who unfairly blamed Cynthia for
"pulling" or "driving" Stephens out of Dublin, claimed that his
departure was a great loss to his "host of friends."[12] Oliver
Gogarty composed a surprisingly serious poem on the
occasion of Stephens' departure, the last two stanzas of
which read:

You passed through all our past worst time, and proved
   yourself no caitiff.
America then listened to a voice too dear for wealth;
Then you went to London where I fear you have gone native;
Too long in a metropolis will tax a poet's health.

It's not as if you had no wit, and cared for recognition;
A mind that lit the Liffey could emblazon all the Thames,
But we're not ourselves without you and we long for coalition;
Oh, half of Erin's energy! What can have happened, James?[13]

Although Stephens missed Dublin, he was able to visit
Stephen MacKenna who had moved to England, he was
often invited to the London house of Lady Ottoline Morrell,
and he soon made many new friends, among them the critic
and translator Samuel Koteliansky. While living in London
he published a second group of short stories, *Etched in Moonlight*
(1928), a book of essays, *On Prose and Verse* (1928), a short
prose piece, *How St. Patrick Saves the Irish* (1931), and several
volumes of poetry.

Between 1925 and 1935 Stephens made at least nine tours
of the United States. These were not pleasurable occasions
but working trips. Stephens traveled second class on board
ship and suffered through long periods without his wife and
family in his efforts to earn money by lecturing. His letters

written in the 1930s from America to his family reflect his loneliness and his desire to return to London. In October 1935, after many lecture stops, he wrote wearily, "I think this public talking is the most hideous form of life or business that can be imagined." When he collapsed of illness on one of the trips, his advice to others was, "never get pneumonia in Chicago."[14]

Throughout his life, earning a living as a writer was a strenuous task, even though Stephens was fortunate enough to have three patrons, John Quinn, Cornelius Sullivan, and W. T. H. Howe. Although AE succeeded in interesting Quinn in Stephens' work to the point that the American lawyer bought several of the writer's manuscripts, including *The Crock of Gold*, the two never met. They exchanged a number of letters, however, in the years between 1913 and 1922, and Stephens was always grateful to Quinn not only for his willingness to purchase the manuscripts but for his interest in Stephens as an artist.[15]

Sullivan helped extensively in financial matters; but Stephens' strongest supporter was W. T. H. Howe, the President of the American Book Company. Howe first invited Stephens to Freelands, his summer home in Kentucky, in 1929 after an exchange of letters that began in 1913. He bought Stephens' manuscripts, he offered at Freelands food, drink, and the company of a burro from Texas, and he arranged for several editorial assignments. By 1935 the relationship was beginning to wear on both parties. Howe complained to Ray Harris that the Irish were an odd group whose love of words and whose whimsicality, insincerity, and propensity to dramatize were not always understandable or interesting.[16] The complaint may have been related to Howe's frustration over not getting Stephens settled down to completing a writing assignment, a book on Byron. Howe did not invite Stephens to Freelands in 1936 or thereafter, another indication of his annoyance. Stephens, on the other hand, must have felt a certain amount of distress over the obligation to sing for his supper, for his visits quickly took on the aspect of entertainment for the guests and copy for the newspapers.

The trips to the United States exhausted him; on several, he was so drained by the exertions of a demanding itinerary that he suffered from severe respiratory infections. Yet he was a great favorite of the female college students who attended his readings. According to one story, when a tall young woman expressed a wish to kiss Stephens because she loved his poetry, he obligingly jumped on a chair so that he could bend down and embrace her. Another ex-student recalls an equally fascinating experience at a reading given at Carleton College:

> It was one of those intimate gatherings to which Honors English students are invited to sit at the feet of the master and listen to him wander, watch him sparkle.
> J. S. was irresistible. His chief maneuver was to make an outrageously unorthodox charge against a literary saint, immediately lose interest in supporting the assertion, and continue with a new, darting attack. He leaned over and recited in my face, "O wild west wind, thou breath of Autumn's being . . ." stopped short and said flatly. "After that, he lost the magic."[17]

The deaths in 1934 and 1935 of two close friends, Stephen MacKenna and AE, brought great sadness. Then on 24 December 1937 his son, James Naoise, was killed in an accident at the age of twenty-eight. The shock of this tragedy, Stephens' recurrent illnesses, and his conviction that he had written enough books combined to bring about almost a total end to his writing career, but another artistic occupation took its place. Stephens had always delighted in conversation; now he found a new and receptive audience. From 1941 until his death he was heard in over seventy talks on the BBC, speaking on poets and poetry, reading verse, and reminiscing about old friends.

Stephens declared himself "an Englishman" on the day Italy entered World War II. He admired the courage of the British people in the face of what other people believed to be an invincible German army and wished to express publicly his approval. During the war years he felt the necessity to live with his wife in Gloucestershire to escape the Blitz; he commuted to London, however, to give his BBC broadcasts. He was awarded the British Civil List Pension in 1942. In 1947, with a grant from the Royal Bounty Fund, he went to Dublin to receive an honorary D. Litt. degree from Dublin University (Trinity College).

His last years were spent wandering about London, stopping in book shops, feeding the pigeons in Trafalgar Square, and fighting off recurrent attacks of illness and syncope. Throughout his life he suffered the results of the malnutrition which marked his youth; between 1920 and 1948 he underwent a series of operations for abdominal problems. Illness in the later stage of his life frequently brought about episodes of unreasoned anger, but he remained devoted to his close friends who sought him out when he finally was confined to his home.

He gave his last BBC broadcast, "Childhood Days: Mogue, or Cows and Kids," on 11 June 1950. Although fate may have denied him the birth on St. Brigid's Day that he claimed, he died on St. Stephen's Day, 26 December 1950.

LITERARY BEGINNINGS

In 1891 when Charles Stewart Parnell died, the politicians whom he had kept in line in a unified party split apart, and the result was decades of petty, divisive, ineffectual politics. With the fall of Parnell the romantic hero, many Irishmen moved away from party issues to other activities; among these were small groups who proposed cultural solutions to the problem of nationhood.

Like other young writers, Stephens found himself drawn into the activities of the best-known non-political movement emerging in the late 1890s, the Irish Literary Revival.[18] He found an immediate sympathy with the goals of the Revival's most prominent member and sometime leader, William Butler Yeats, who believed that Irish artists and writers could serve the intellectual and spiritual needs of Ireland, that with a cultural life the Irish could have a nationality, and that the people needed a new literature of the highest aesthetic quality which would be based on Irish characters, actions, and themes.

Yeats and Stephens' mentor, AE, were members of the Dublin Hermetic Society and the Theosophical Society, two groups dedicated to discussion of Eastern philosophy and the occult. This fascination with the occult was shared by Stephens and other artists who were excited by the prospect of understanding the past and predicting a new, "purer" future. Through study, the ancient and medieval world might be explained, and an ethereal purification of the mind and soul might replace the meaningless, material world of Dublin in the late nineteenth century. The Theosophical movement attracted many Irish writers, among them Yeats, AE, John Eglinton, and Stephens. Yeats said that he was "much among the Theosophists" at this time, and he thought that his admiration for them was in part an escape from the "restlessness" of his mind.[19]

AE and Yeats met in 1883; by 1890 both were studying Irish folklore, Theosophy, and spiritualism. Approximately seven years later, AE wrote Yeats that "the gods" had returned to Ireland and "a new Avatar" was about to appear.[20] Although AE, Yeats, and even George Moore, at one time or another aspired to the role of Irish avatar, the period passed without tumultuous event. Stephens did not forget AE's prediction, however, and in 1912 brought the gods back to Ireland in *The Crock of Gold*.

As a disciple and friend of AE, Stephens attended his mentor's Sunday evening parties at which discussions frequently centered around mystical doctrine, and he was present at some of the Hermetic Society meetings. In 1912 he reviewed *The Wisdom of the West*, a set of lectures by James Cousins in which Celtic myths were interpreted in Theosophical terms, and he was reading Madame Blavatsky's *The Secret Doctrine* during Easter Week 1916. While he never joined the Dublin Lodge, there are certain recurrent themes in Stephens' works which are specifically Theosophical: an interest in prophetic dreams, a presentation of the eternal conflict between good and evil, and an emphasis on the triune nature of man. In *The Charwoman's Daughter*, Mrs. Makebelieve assures Mary that dreams hold more than is "generally understood," and she reports a dream about her brother which is, in part, prophetic. As he ends this story the narrator informs the reader that "next to good the most valuable factor in life is evil," and in the second novel we are told that "out of evil good must ultimately come." Both lines reflect Madame Blavatsky's belief that evil is the inner lining of good. Caitilin's choice between two gods in *The Crock of Gold* is also in keeping with Theosophical doctrine if she is seen as a symbol of the soul first in a poor union with the body and then in the proper union with the spirit. Two of Stephens' short stories, "Desire" and "Etched in Moonlight," treat dreams as revelatory of the future and of a past existence. One work which draws heavily upon Theosophical concepts is *The Demi-Gods*; but Stephens utilized concepts from Eastern thought throughout his writing, particularly in his late-period poetry.

Stephens was also influenced by that segment of the nationalist movement represented by John O'Leary, the imprisoned and exiled Fenian who had returned to Ireland in late 1884. Unlike most Fenians, O'Leary was more interested in culture than revolution. He gave speeches in Dublin urging the study of Ireland's history, literature, geography, and mythology. His beliefs soon brought Yeats to his home, along with Douglas Hyde, Katharine Tynan, and Maud Gonne. Yeats, Tynan, and Hyde published *Poems and Ballads of Young Ireland*, a collection of writings by young Irish writers, dedicated to John O'Leary and the Young Ireland Societies, in 1888. In December 1891 Yeats helped to found the Irish Literary Society of London, and in May 1892 he established the National Literary Society in Dublin. The objectives of these groups were the same: to publicize Irish poetry, folklore, and mythology.

Yeats' first published book of poetry, *The Wanderings of Oisin*, was a retelling or, to use Stephens' word, "reincarnation" of Gaelic legend. Because Yeats believed that if the Irish people could be reached through literature and art, a period of spiritual awakening would take place, he pictured Ireland as a poor old woman (the *Shan Van Vocht*) or a beautiful young girl who would be queen once more when Irishmen became as chivalrous and death-defying as the legendary hero Cúchulinn; Yeats' definitive portrait of this theme was his play, *Cathleen ni Houlihan*.

Stephens' versions of the same story are found in his first three novels. In each work a beautiful woman, representing Ireland, is championed by an Irishman who is in turn a young patriot, a Gaelic deity, and an angel with an Irish name. Many of Stephens' works reflect his dedication to the literary reawakening of Ireland. After he had soaked himself "to the scalp and beyond in the older Irish writers," he wrote his finest contributions to the Literary Movement: *Reincarnations* (1918), *Irish Fairy Tales* (1920), *Deirdre* (1923), and *In the Land of Youth* (1924).

The results of the Literary Revival were often collaborative efforts: plays jointly conceived by Yeats and Lady Gregory, by Lady Gregory and Douglas Hyde, or by Yeats and George Moore; short stories written by Moore with Stephens' help; poems of Stephens edited by AE. The acknowledged leader, Yeats presided over all the proceedings, making suggestions, modifying others' writing, and often serving as the center of heated controversy. That there was controversy is evident from Moore's *Hail and Farewell*. In this work, Moore sets forth a picture of the Literary Revival which portrays the Irish writers fighting in a small arena the inevitable political antagonisms that beset Ireland. Quarrels, jealousies, and divisions were the daily order on the Irish scene even for the writers of the Literary Revival, who were so full of larger dreams of unity and fulfillment. The much-beloved AE defined a literary movement as "five or six people who live in the same town and hate each other cordially."[21]

By 1914 Edward Martyn, one of the founders of the Literary Theatre, was attacking his former colleagues, claiming that Yeats had "a dictatorial manner which is irresistible with the considerable bevy of female and male mediocrities interested in intellectual things" and that Lady Gregory was "not intellectually profound." By this time he had organized a new group, the Irish Theatre Company, to encourage the production of "native Irish drama other than the peasant species."[22]

James Joyce and others agreed with Martyn's position that the emphasis on peasant drama was unfortunate. In "The Day of the Rabblement" Joyce severely criticized the Irish Literary Theatre for not producing works by Ibsen, Strindberg, and other European playwrights and accused the founders of "courting the favour of the multitude." Stephens concurred. In a lecture, "Irish Idiosyncrasies," which was printed in 1910 in *Sinn Féin*, he wrote:

I deplore and reprobate the present glorification of the peasant. I am very sick of peasants. The Abbey Theatre has given us three or four years of undiluted peasant, so has the Theatre of Ireland, so have many of our journals. We are beginning to wear our peasantry as consciously as we do our ancient greatness and our heroes. It is ridiculous every city man of us marching about with a country man pinned in his hat.[23]

Critical of themselves and others, the writers of the Literary Revival found their targets in the literature, religion, politics, and daily life of Ireland. At best, they presented a new national literature which, as Yeats demanded, was of the highest aesthetic quality; at worst, their writings were precious, misty, overly sentimental, leading James Joyce to coin the phrase, "the cultic twalette." It was in this milieu that Stephens began his writing career.

As a young writer he felt that he should read other authors who were considered masters in the field, and thus he stopped reading his favorites — Ouida, Marie Corelli, and Arthur Conan Doyle — and began on Dickens, Browning, Thackeray, Hardy, Meredith, and Wilde. He found Thackeray a bore and Meredith "cruel" to his characters. He liked Hardy, calling him a great "peasant writer," and he enjoyed George Moore's Irish works, including *The Lake*. The readings led him to a career, for from Browning and Wilde he gained the desire to write poetry and fiction, and the career led to life-long associations with other Irish writers. It is in these relationships that certain aspects of his life and work are revealed.

His closest friend, AE, served as mentor, literary agent, and critic. In 1908, AE wrote Katharine Tynan that he had "discovered" Stephens and was trying to find a publisher for Stephens' first book of poetry. Successful in this pursuit, he next sent a copy of *Insurrections* to John Quinn in hopes of interesting Quinn in his protégé. By 1913 AE thought of Stephens as his "boon companion": he advised Stephens to read the *Bhagavadgita* and the *Upanishads*; his monologues inspired the series called "The Old Philosopher" in *Sinn Féin* and the character of the Philosopher in *The Crock of Gold*; he arranged introductions of friends in Paris when Stephens left Dublin to live in France; he offered money and help to Mrs. Stephens on more than one occasion upon hearing of Stephens' illnesses; he worried over Stephens' apparent stoppage of writing in 1925 and scolded him in the 1930s for wasting his genius on talking instead of writing.

George Moore used Stephens as a sounding board for his opinions and an editor for three of his short stories.[24] He attempted to persuade Stephens to leave Ireland for England some years before Stephens actually left. He also offered suggestions on subject matter for future works: the life history of an Irish tinker, a servant girl who follows "the lure of vagrancy," parish priests, but "no gods or angels."

Stephens' first meeting with James Joyce was a jousting session. Joyce's early opinion of Stephens' artistic ability has been recorded in a letter to his brother Stanislaus in which Stephens is labeled "my rival, the latest Irish genius."[25] In *Ulysses* Stephen Dedalus overhears a conversation at the library in which there are references to George Russell's plan to gather together "a sheaf of our younger poets' verses" and to James Stephens' "doing some clever sketches," a not very complimentary remark — and not very accurate, since Stephens' "sketches" did not appear in *Sinn Féin* until 1907. Stephens' recollection of their introduction and conversation in a Dublin pub includes his having told Joyce that he should adopt the motto, "Rejoice and be exceedingly bad."[26] In letters to Thomas Bodkin, W. T. H. Howe, Lewis Chase, and John Quinn written between 1914 and 1922, Stephens continued his attack on Joyce's work, finding only *Chamber Music* an acceptable work of art.[27]

After a fifteen-year period notable for a lack of direct communication between the feuding parties, it was Joyce who began a friendship in 1927 which led to bottles of wine, mutual birthday parties, and the greatest gift of all, recognition of Stephens' artistic worth in his suggestion that Stephens finish *Finnegans Wake* if he could not do so.[28] In the "Anna Livia Plurabelle" section of "Work in Progress" which he published in November 1927, Joyce referred directly to Stephens:

for Seumas, thought little, a crown he feels big. . . .[29]

Shortly afterward he made the first of several requests that Stephens "take over the book," and discussion of this plan continued for two years.

Joyce also tried unsuccessfully to persuade Stephens of Ibsen's artistic worth, recommended a physician for Stephens to consult regarding his glandular condition, and provided the opportunity for Stephens to substitute for him as a lecturer at the Third International Book Fair in Florence in 1928. Stephens reciprocated by calling "Anna Livia Plurabelle" "the greatest prose ever written by a man," and by responding to Joyce's talk of persecutions with the cry, "You are a king, and a king should have an eye to see and an arm to strike!"[30]

Stephens' friendship with Stephen MacKenna lasted from 1908 to MacKenna's death in 1934. They exchanged and shared ideas, books, letters, visits, notes on guitar playing, and concertina lessons. The writer Seumas O'Sullivan [James Starkey] also knew Stephens for a number of years beginning with an introduction by Arthur Griffith in 1906. O'Sullivan and Stephens were close friends during the early period of Stephens' writing, then drifted apart although they continued to exchange letters and occasional visits until the 1930s.

To Thomas Bodkin, Stephens turned for friendship, moral support, occasional financial assistance, and literary advice. He wrote frequently to Bodkin during his stay in Paris, confiding his lack of progress in the ability to speak French, his feelings of awe upon viewing Gertrude Stein's collection of modern art, and his hopes concerning his various writing projects. He volunteered to edit and criticize Bodkin's manuscript for a book, *May It Please Your Lordships*, and submitted his own poetry to Bodkin for his impressions. It was Bodkin who suggested that Stephens apply for a position in the National Gallery of Ireland, and who, in turn, Stephens hoped would obtain the position of Director in 1916 when Walter Strickland resigned. Bodkin was not appointed Director until 1927, after Stephens had resigned his position. By this time their friendship had waned because of disagreements over decisions made by the Director for whom Stephens had worked, Captain Robert Langton Douglas.

A boon companion in his London years was Samuel Koteliansky ("Kot"), a translator, an editor, and a friend of the circle which included D. H. Lawrence, Katherine Mansfield, John Middleton Murry, Virginia and Leonard Woolf, Beatrice Lady Glenavy, Lady Ottoline Morrell, and others. Ridgeway's in London was the meeting place, on Wednesdays, of various members of the group in the 1930s. When Stephens met Kot, they immediately became friends and colleagues. Kot was an admirer of *The Crock of Gold*; Stephens provided a foreword for Kot's translation of Vasili Vasilyevich Rozanov's *Fallen Leaves, Bundle One*; Kot's despair over the suicide of a friend and his deepening depression over the growing shadow of Hitler over Europe was at least one influence on the writing of "The Lion of Judah," a poem in Stephens' *Kings and the Moon*. According to Lady Glenavy, Stephens said, "the greatest book on English literature which has *never* been written is by Kot."[31] Koteliansky and Stephens were admirably suited: they were perfectionists in the art of conversation, they held strong opinions on political and literary issues — and even stronger ones on people — and like most writers in exile they were able to gather around them the artistic, the brilliant, and the wealthy people of their day. During the Blitz, when Stephens and his family had moved to Woodside Chapel to avoid the bombings, he wrote frequently to his friend, declaring his friendship:

I wish I could see you every Wednesday. I wish I could see you every day of the week. I wish that U and I, and D, and whatever other alphebeticals you would elect for, could be meeting together once a week, and lunching together once a day, and dining together every night; and that, thereon, we all went to bed together. How delicious t'would be, then, for us all to breakfast together: and, thereon, to start getting ready to lunch, and dine, and bed and board with ourselves, and with none others whatever. As far as the world is concerned I am indifferent — but, I like my loves![32]

Their only point of violent disagreement must have been on the subject of Cynthia Stephens. There is no hint of this matter in their letters, but Lady Glenavy reports an incident after Stephens' death in which Kot and Cynthia battle each other under the guise of polite conversation. Cynthia wins, by showing Kot a love poem written about her many years previously by Stephens. But Kot has the last word, striding around the room after Cynthia leaves, opening windows and doors and exclaiming, "the very air is contaminated!" As

Lady Glenavy, a startled witness to this confrontation points out, "Kot's hates and prejudices were no ordinary emotions."[33]

Although AE was, early on, devoted to Stephens as a poet, Yeats was not. He once referred to Stephens as one of AE's "canaries," and when AE worked to achieve the publication of a volume of Stephens' poetry, he said, "for me the aesthetical question; for you, my dear friend, the philanthropic." Late in life Stephens recalled with amusement a set of defeats in mock battle with four of the figures of literary Ireland:

> ... Yeats and I were the only poets with good manners that ever lived. When he had finished a poem I always asked him to say it again and when I had finished one he as scrupulously invited me to repeat *the last verse.*

> "Jamesy," said MacKenna, "your poetry is the worst in the world, and your prose is getting to be nearly as good as that."

> Here Joyce woke up: he exploded moderately into conversation. He turned his chin and his specs at me, and away down at me, and confided the secret to me that he had read my two books; that, grammatically, I did not know the difference between a semi-colon and a colon: that my knowledge of Irish life was non-Catholic and, so, non-existent, and that I should give up writing and take to a good job like shoe-shining as a more promising profession.

> "What are you working at now, Stephens?" said [Moore].
> "This morning," I replied, "I translated 'The County of Mayo' from the Gaelic."
> "That is my country," said he, "and so I am interested. But, my dear Stephens, that poem has been translated so many times already that you are wasting your — ah — talent, yes, perhaps talent, on a job that every literate person in Ireland has done before you."
> "Why, Moore?" said I.
> Here he broke in: "Don't you think, Stephens, that I have come to the years in which younger men should address me as 'Mr. Moore'?"[34]

When reading these hilarious accounts, the reader must

remember that Yeats was an admirer of Stephens' fiction, that Joyce, Moore, and MacKenna sought Stephens out as a writer, editor, and critic, and that Stephens was a great storyteller whose tales about himself at times rivaled his fiction for imagination and humor.

In Stephens' writing there are hints of his past life which we may take seriously, if we can. He claims that his first job was as a messenger for a theatrical agency. All well and good, but what is to be made of another claim in the same piece — that a rhinoceros once fell in love with his shoes?[35] There are other stories Stephens told about his youth. In *A Penny in the Clouds*, Austin Clarke recalled that Stephens said that he was a foundling who walked the streets and chased the ducks in St. Stephen's Green in order to steal bits of bread from them. Lord Grey claimed it was a swan which Stephens fought for a piece of bread; in a BBC broadcast, Stephens said it was a terrier.[36] Lady Gregory heard a tale of Stephens' pinching tomatoes from a street vendor, but for the adventure of stealing, not out of starvation. AE said that as a young man Stephens was hungry and homeless for over a year and was saved from starving by a woman street vendor; George Moore called the vendor an "applewoman"; Lennox Robinson told people that the woman was a prostitute.[37]

Stephens did not help his critics to investigate the details of his early life. He would not settle the dispute over his birth date or the conflicting rumors about his youth. At most, he offered his works as reflections of his life. In "The Old Woman's Money," for example, he claimed that a book is "a lecture on the state of [the author's] mental health"; in "An Essay in Cubes," he suggested that there are two stories in every book, the tale for the reader and the story about himself which "the writer has not been able to keep out of his pages."[38] In the latter essay, he also suggests that biography should be based on a psychological analysis of the works of the artist, that the character of the artist is in the printed pages not his letters.

Only in a few places was Stephens more specific, for example, this section from a letter to Lewis Chase:

As to my people. I am reduced to claiming the entire

Irish nation for ancestry, my own parents died when I was about six years of age, and I have not met one of my own clann since that time. I went to work about sixteen, and was discharged from, and discharged myself from innumerable situations. I would sooner be a corpse than a clerk, and I have been a hungry man many, many times. . . . Of education I got the ordinary stuffing provided by most schools twenty years ago. I learned geography and grammar and the bible [—] things like that, and forgot them a great deal easier than I learned them. That quickness in forgetting is a kind of activity also, I suppose. . . . The dislike I got of teachers has lasted to this day, coupled with a dislike for clergymen and policemen and politicians.[39]

But Stephens also wrote to Chase that his life could be found in his books, and it is true that there are glimpses of Stephens and his family in the writings. An early story, "Miss Arabella Hennessy," contains a young man who, like the youthful Stephens, loves equally talk and athletic stunts. The lodgers who appear in *Here Are Ladies* and *The Charwoman's Daughter* are other pictures of Stephens as a young man: thin, none too neat, energetic, and loquacious.

Hilary Pyle may be correct that Stephens' father died when he was two years old; however, in an unpublished "memory" of childhood, Stephens recalls that when he was ten, he felt the "strangeness" of his father, and then adds, "ah me, my poor pop went and died — they all do."[40] Stephens' youthful protagonists who are missing at least one parent — Mary Makebelieve, Caitilin Ni Murrachu, Mary Mac Cann, Deirdre, Fionn, Oisín, Etain, and Nera — may hold some aspects of the young Stephens. Moreover, if his mother remarried after her husband's death, the effect of that remarriage upon Stephens may be reflected in the following passage from *Irish Fairy Tales* about Fionn's mother; the commentary does not appear in Stephens' saga sources.

As for Muirne she must have loved her lord; or she may have been terrified in truth of the sons of Morna and for Fionn; but it is so also, that if a woman loves her second husband she can dislike all that reminds her of the first one.[41]

The woman in "Hunger" recalls a tale about a mother who kept her crippled child in a box when she had to leave home for work. Austin Clarke attributed Stephens' "twisted frame, goitrous throat, rickety limbs" to malnutrition caused by such a deprived childhood.[42] Clarke's comment is peculiar, for despite his short stature (he was about five foot in height) Stephens was a good gymnast and a sturdy man. The only connection between "Hunger" and its author's life may be that in it the woman's husband dies when her children are quite young.

The Policeman's behavior at the end of *The Charwoman's Daughter* may be drawn from the unreasonable jealousy of Cynthia Stephens' first husband when the attractiveness of his wife caused other men to admire her. Certainly, Mary Makebelieve's authoritative pronouncements on clothing reflect Cynthia's talent as a dressmaker. Mrs. Stephens' physical and personal attributes may be found in a number of Stephens' heroines: she was as lovely, clever, strong, and determined as Deirdre, Mary Mac Cann, and Caitilin Ni Murrachu. Iris and Seumas Stephens were models for Brigid and Seumas Beg, the young children in *The Crock of Gold*, although Stephens also saw himself as little James.

His stepdaughter, Iris Wise, has said that Stephens' response to questions concerning his birth date was, "my life began when I started writing." The man and the artist are inextricably connected in the published works. They may be found, too, in brief, impromptu poems which, although they were never meant to be published, reveal Stephens' delight in writing poetry and in earthly and familial pleasures. Here, for example, are a thank-you note to his friend Moses Strauss for two bottles of "dew" and a note written on a postcard when his children were young:

> My dear Mose:
> I got those,
> Those lovely two,
> Sent me from you:
> Sweet as the rose
> Are they;

And comforting
Like anything,
All woes away.
Seumas is an egg
Iris is a rasher
Daddy wags his leg
And our mammy is a dasher.[43]

Over the years he perfected an early talent for the outrageous remark. His pronouncements to reporters became justly famous, for example: "there are two things in the world that give beauty to a woman — a squint and a mustache."[44]

Whatever the media, Stephens believed that an artist was always engaged in a portrait of himself. In his broadcasts for the BBC, he revealed himself in what he had to say in praise of his contemporaries: he admired Arthur Griffith's resolute manner and strength of character, Synge's love of the countryside, Yeats' "passionate utterance," MacKenna's remarkable ability as a conversationalist, AE's varied activities and his prodigious capability as a monologist, Shaw's cogent arguments, and Joyce's purity of language. All of these qualities Stephens possessed.

From the statements of others, final aspects of a portrait of Stephens can be sketched. According to the descriptions of him given by his contemporaries, he looked like "the King of the Leprechauns," "a drolly wise gnome," a "pre-Celtic" being, and "a powerful, tiny elf."[45] Katherine Tynan once said that Padraic Colum's face was that of a young man going into a wood. Austin Clarke responded that Stephens had the mysterious look of a young man coming out of a wood. He loved pancakes, accordion playing, mice, chickens, ducks, calves, fleas, and toads; he was fascinated by the love life of the spiders he observed at Eversleigh; he liked to recite his poetry out loud; he was always ready to talk, and on any subject. And he disliked only three things: meanness, cowardice, and exile from Ireland.

2 The Dance of Life

THE CHARWOMAN'S DAUGHTER (1912)

According to Stephens, the original inspiration for *The Charwoman's Daughter*, was Oscar Wilde's *A House of Pomegranates*. By reading "about twenty pages" of Wilde's novel, he reached his first "illuminating" conclusion: "the art of prose-writing does not really need a murder to carry it."[1] He explains that this thought led to a second realization that a novel need not be a philosophical work, that it need not be infused by its author with artificial thought, but rather that it succeeds or fails on its prose style:

> Writing can be quite good, and yet have no violence whatever in it. It can be powerful on a very minimum of action. It can be wise on a very minimum of thought. It can exist by writing alone . . . .[2]

Having rejected murder and philosophy as suitable topics, Stephens says that he simply began writing "with the idea of doing a something which I conceived that Wilde had tried, and perhaps failed to do."[3]

He writes that when he began his first novel, his wife served as a model for his heroine and that he found the model for her mother (Mrs. Makebelieve) within himself. The latter remark, which might prove surprising to his reader, is explained in terms both comic and philosophic:

> Indeed, I discovered that a patient examination of myself
> could produce the model of anything whatever, from a cake
> of soap to an hippogriff.[4]

> A work of art will rarely fail by reason of its author's intellec-
> tual poverty — it can fail when the identity between subject
> and object has broken: It fails when the artist cannot will
> to be his matter, and, so, cannot will his matter to be.
> . . . To identify the object; to fuse self and not-self, is the
> privilege, and is the first and the last duty, of an artist.[5]

Thus Stephens' first novel was begun with several motivations:
it was a new writer's challenge of a master, an artist's act
of "universal self-identification" with his material, and an effort
to produce "good writing."

The work resulting from these challenges, *The Charwoman's
Daughter*, is a remarkably harmonious blend of disparate styles
and genres. It ranges in tone from whimsy to objectivity, from
sentimentality to "philosophizing," and in approach from passages reminiscent of the nineteenth-century novelist to those
peculiar to Stephens alone. At various times and in varying
degrees it is a fairy tale about two characters called the Makebelieves, a realistic look at life in the Dublin slums, and a psychological analysis of the relationship between a widowed mother
and her daughter.

The heroine of the novel, Mary Makebelieve, lives with her
mother, a charwoman, in a room at the top of a building
not unlike the turrets in which fairy princesses are generally
hidden. At the beginning of the story the tenement room is
described in terms of what Mary sees — its cracks, its faded
wallpaper, its intrinsic dinginess — but the main piece of furni-
ture in the room, at least as far as Mary is concerned, is
a cracked looking-glass. She and her mother stand before this
mirror looking at their images, as ladies in imaginary tales
often do. Mary waits in this tenement room for a "strange,
beautiful man" to come and take her away. According to
Mary, the man might appear in one of three areas, the forest,
the seacoast, or the plain — all favorite places for heroines

to find their lovers and places to be found in Stephens' later reworkings of the ancient Gaelic stories of Oisín's mother, Becfola, and Becuma in *Irish Fairy Tales* — but hardly places frequented by people from Dublin's slums. Mary's romantic nature is matched by her mother's fantasies. Mrs. Makebelieve does not dream of a knight on horseback; but she does imagine suitors for her daughter: elegant young men who have white hands (Mrs. Makebelieve's hands are reddened), speak French, and bow often "with their hats almost touching the ground."

Mary has long, shining, "light gold" hair, her face is small and white, and her eyes are grey. Mrs. Makebelieve's face is "old, old ivory," her hands are "all knuckle," her nose is a "great strong beak"; unlike Mary's, her eyes and her hair are black. Of course a daughter need not resemble her mother, but it would seem that Stephens has something more symbolical in mind. Certain personality traits of Mary and her mother can be distinguished which suggest a mode of characterization common in Victorian fiction and in some folk tales: Mary, the blond, is sweet and docile; her mother, a brunette, is temperamental and violent in her opinions.[6]

The opening of the novel, then, gives us a modern Cinderella with a testy but benevolent mother or, perhaps, a Snow White with one grumpy dwarf. But these fairy-tale components are all within the first chapters of the novel. After that, the gauzy backdrop is raised into the wings where it remains until the last pages of the book. For if Stephens' description of Mary and her desires is idealized, his description of her mother's thoughts, work, and life is wholly realistic.

In keeping with her physical appearance, Mrs. Makebelieve's view of poverty is quite without illusion. When she sees destitute people on the streets, she wants to believe that they receive charity, but she is reminded of their economic straits when she undresses at night and sees her own "lean ribs of humanity." Although she professes her "willingness and ability to undertake with success any form of work in which a woman could be eminent," she knows that life is a terrifying and constant search for food.

Present in several passages are Stephens' attempts to expound his own theories through the character for whom he served as a model. These sections include an analysis of Mrs. Makebelieve's troubled relationships with her clients, her belief in humanity, and her speculation on the extremities and hardships of the poor. Honest about others and about herself, Mrs. Makebelieve takes no pains to conceal from her employers her views on the inequality of men, and these remarks, along with others concerning the appearances and morals of her clients, inevitably lead to dismissal. Mrs. Makebelieve is not opposed to the rich, but to people who "order others about." What she demands is what Stephens asked for in "The Insurrection of '98," an essay written for *Sinn Féin* in 1908: justice, not from God but from other human beings. She is joined in a later portion of the story by a young lodger, a character also identifiable with Stephens, who condemns landlords, policemen, employers, and others who exploit the poor.

Mrs. Makebelieve's relationship with her daughter, however, is not realistic. Mary is sixteen, but she is not allowed to work. She spends her days walking and looking at "the world" while her mother scrubs floors. When they are home together, her mother directs Mary to wear her hair down and to walk around the room in her petticoats "to heighten the illusion of girlishness." It angers Mrs. Makebelieve to see that Mary's figure is becoming that of a woman; she would like her daughter to be a child forever. Mrs. Makebelieve has named her daughter's fingers Tom Tumkins, Willie Winkles, Long Daniel, Bessie Bobtail, and Little Dick-Dick. The names are a clear indication of Mrs. Makebelieve's wish to prolong Mary's infancy. "She was the mother and Mary was the baby, and she could not bear to have her motherhood hindered even in play."

Mary is also obsessed with hands, but while her concern matches in intensity that of her mother, it differs in direction. She has a deep-seated fear of being struck by a man, or, although this is a less frequent fear, by her mother. When she sees the Policeman, she thinks about the "immense shattering blow" his fist could give, and when she meets and talks with him in the park she wonders if policemen are ever slapped. Her first assessment of the man is couched in sexual terms: "she did not dare venture within reach of that powerful organism"; when she leaves the park after their first meeting, the policeman takes off his hat, and Mary notes in a "subterranean and half-conscious fashion" that this is the first time a man has ever "uncovered before her."

Mary's walks not only lead to revelation of her preoccupations, but they are a means for Stephens to describe familiar Dublin streets, parks, and faces. Grafton, Nassau, and Suffolk Streets and the People's Gardens of the Phoenix Park are viewed along with Mary's and Stephens' favorite park, St. Stephen's Green. George Russell (AE) delighted in telling his friends that he was the furiously-talking tall bearded man on the street whose overcoat "looked as though it has been put on with a shovel." Mary sees three other famous Dubliners on her walks: Yeats is the thin man who smiles "secretly" to himself; Synge is the pale-faced man who makes Mary feel that she knew him before; and George Moore is the detached man with the bleak and aloof smile.

But it is the Policeman who attracts her attention and appears to her to be the long-awaited Prince Charming. The wise reader is not as convinced as Mary, however, for policemen are never heroes in Stephens' writing. The police in *The Crock of Gold* are inept and their sergeant in charge is ponderous, a quality he shares with the "gigantic" policeman in "Miss Arabella Hennessy." And in *Arthur Griffith*, Stephens tells, with obvious approval, a story about Griffith's refusal to turn over to the police three young hooligans who had harassed him on the street because he could not "deliver any person into the hands of what he politically considered was rank injustice."[7] Although the knees of Mary's policeman remind her of those of a statue of a god, he will be revealed as neither a monument of solidity nor god-like.[8]

The Policeman's wry description of criminals and his dispassionate report on the lives of the poor presage his later conflict with Mrs. Makebelieve, whose views on poverty are understandably more sympathetic. When not giving Mary reports on his bravery, the Policeman asks questions about her background. Although Mary rejoices in his interest, she senses his feelings toward the slum-dwellers, and she feels compelled to lie to him; she tells him that her mother is a dressmaker.

While Mary pursues her flirtation with the Policeman, her mother goes about her work. Like the description in Chapter I of the Makebelieve's room, the passage on Mrs. Makebelieve's employer's house in Chapter XI is both detailed and comic. Stephens and Mrs. Makebelieve make fun of the O'Connors' belongings and, in particular, their art collection:

> ... there was a plaque whereon a young lady dressed in
> a sky-blue robe crossed by means of well-defined stepping-
> stones a thin but furious stream; the middle distance was
> embellished by a cow, and the horizon sustained two white
> lambs, a brown dog, a fountain, and a sun-dial. ... two
> [pictures] portrayed saintly but emaciated personages sitting
> in peculiarly disheartening wildernesses (each wilderness con-
> tained one cactus plant and a camel). One of these personages
> stared fixedly at a skull; the other personage looked with
> intense firmness away from a lady of scant charms in a
> white and all-too-insufficient robe: above the robe a segment
> of the lady's bosom was hinted at bashfully — it was probably
> this the personage looked firmly away from.[9]

When Mrs. Makebelieve, who has seemed a woman of
strength to her daughter, grows ill, Stephens draws upon materials he has used previously and will use again for his narrative
passages. Mrs. Makebelieve's symptoms are those of Michael
O'Neill, the clerk in "The Man Who Was Afraid," a story
written in 1909 and later incorporated into *The Crock of Gold*.[10]
Like O'Neill, Mrs. Makebelieve fears not the malady but its
consequences, the terrors of being without wages. She is also
frantic when she realizes that her daughter must go to work
in her place, but typically, she worries first about the loss
of Mary's dependency and only secondarily about the life of
poverty her daughter faces.

Mary's response to unpleasant events is also revealed during
the crisis. When she sees the Policeman at the theatre with
another girl, she goes to the park rather than bringing food
home to her invalid mother; this response is a transference
of her anger toward the Policeman, but it also reveals her
anger with her mother, whose illness has caused her to face
the reality of poverty. Her guilt over her shirking of familial
responsibility takes the form of wanting to "baby" her mother
when she returns home; so too she wishes, for a brief period
of time, to cuddle the Policeman.

Although Stephens is optimistic enough to believe that "to
a young person even work is an adventure, and anything which
changes the usual current of life is welcome," Mary is not

ready to be a charwoman. Her immature nature is revealed
first when she christens the boots in the O'Connor household
with names out of bedtime stories: Grubtoes, Sloucher, Thump-
thump, Hoppit, Twitter, Hideaway, and Fairybell. The names
of the boots, of course, recall her mother's names for Mary's
fingers. After the shock of seeing the Policeman while she is
scrubbing his aunt's floor, Mary walks home as a child would,
taking care to avoid stepping on cracks in the pavement, and
when she arrives, she joins in the rollicking games played by
Mrs. Cafferty's young children.

Mrs. Cafferty, the Makebelieve's garrulous neighbor, is a
picturesque figure burdened with the problems created by having six energetic children:

> An infant and a fireplace act upon each other like magnets;
> a small boy is always trying to eat a kettle or a piece of
> coal or the backbone of a herring; a little girl and a slop-buck-
> et are in immediate contact; the baby has a knife in its
> mouth; the twin is on the point of swallowing a marble,
> or is trying to wash itself in the butter, or the cat is about
> to take a nap on its face.[11]

But Mrs. Cafferty is more than a comic figure. She enables
Stephens to launch a philosophical discourse on the conflicts
between husbands and wives. Indeed, Stephens seems unwilling
to turn the conversation over to Mary and Mrs. Cafferty,
and instead addresses his audience directly in the manner of
Thackeray or Meredith. Certainly these lines are Stephens',
not Mrs. Cafferty's:

> The mysteries of death and birth occupy women far more
> than is the case with men, to whom political and mercantile
> speculations are more congenial. With immediate buying and
> selling, and all the absolute forms of exchange and barter,
> women are deeply engaged, so that the realities of trade
> are often more intelligible to them than to many merchants.
> If men understood domestic economy half as well as women
> do, then their political economy and their entire consequent
> statecraft would not be the futile muddle which it is.[12]

When Mary and Mrs. Cafferty walk in the streets of Dublin

on their shopping expedition, Mary sees the Policeman on duty, and although the memory of seeing him at Mrs. O'Connor's house has become an "event of her childhood," she again fears his "great" hand. When she meets him again, Mary senses a change in his behavior. The man has become overly familiar in manner because, on visiting his aunt Mrs. O'Connor, he has discovered Mary in the act of washing a floor, "whence it appears that there is really only one grave and debasing vice in the world, and that is poverty." The inevitable confrontation scene ends at a frenzied pitch in which Stephens aptly conveys Mary's sexual anxieties: she thinks the Policeman wants "to eat her up," his arms seem like "great red spiders" squeezing her, and his bristly moustache spikes her "to death."

The dire economic straits of the Cafferty family bring about the necessity of taking in a lodger. The new lodger turns out to be a good-natured, talkative young man who is "thin as a lath," a description which recalls the young clerk in the story in *Here Are Ladies* entitled, "Three Heavy Husbands — I"; both characters are certainly based on Stephens himself.

Mary's first reaction upon meeting the lodger is annoyance because she feels that she is not suitably attired. She has become involved in discussions with her mother about clothes, an interest which is not new but which growing maturity has intensified. While Mary's mind is dwelling on clothing, the Policeman's is ruminating on her failure to accept his embraces. His thoughts are very direct and violent: he wants to wound then heal her. The intermingling of love and hate is a topic pursued throughout Stephens' fiction. His representation of the Policeman's ambivalent thoughts is remarkably like that of George Meredith, a novelist with whom he can be compared. In Meredith's *The Egoist*, for example, Sir Willoughby reacts to his fiancée's coldness by trying to wound her; furthermore, he takes particular exception to the fact that Clara "prattles" away to Colonel de Craye who is "as Irish as could be."[13] The Policeman is similarly enraged by the sight of Mary chatting easily with the patriotic young lodger, and the lodger inevitably becomes the target of the Policeman's aggressions.

If the young man is a surrogate victim for the Policeman, he is also a surrogate child for Mrs. Makebelieve. She is willing to acknowledge Mary as a maturing adolescent because she thinks of the lodger as a child, a boy to replace the little girl she is losing. The young man also contributes to Mary's emotional development. At first he unwittingly feeds her fears by telling her stories of people being hit, but when he in turn is beaten by the Policeman, she is able both to identify with him and to be protective of him. Thus, the lodger's presence allows Mrs. Makebelieve to relinquish her hold over Mary and to accept her daughter as a young woman and, at the same time, allows Mary to act out her own maternal instincts, instincts which she was unable to develop in her relationship with her mother or with the Policeman. For Stephens, this is a happy moment: his ideal woman is both comrade and mother to a man.

But the lodger is not merely a means of demonstrating displacement and transference. This young man is the voice for a concern for the poor and for Ireland, subjects which play an important part in all Stephens' writings. One of his earliest essays, "Builders," contains the lament recalled by the lodger: "Alas, alas, and alas!/For the once proud people of Bamba."[14] The plight of the poor Dubliners brought forth "Fifty Pounds a Year and a Pension," "A Street," and "Nature," angry poems in *Insurrections*. The essays, "The Seoinin," "Patriotism and Parochial Politics," and "Irish Englishmen," and a short story, "Mrs. Maurice M'Quillan," are other examples of his writings on economics and patriotism.

Like Mrs. Makebelieve, the young man is opposed to slum landlords, soldiers, and despotic employers. Although Stephens says he dismissed Wilde's *House of Pomegranates* after "about twenty pages," one wonders if he read far enough to come across this section:

"In War," answered the weaver, "the strong make slaves of the weak, and in peace the rich make slaves of the poor. We must work to live, and they give us such mean wages that we die. . . . our children fade away before their time, and the faces of those we love become hard and evil . . . Through our sunless lanes creeps Poverty with her hungry eyes, and Sin with his sodden face follows close behind her. Misery wakes us in the morning, and Shame sits with us at night."[15]

Not only the thoughts of the lodger and Mrs. Makebelieve,

but those of Angus Óg in *The Crock of Gold*, Stephens' next
novel, recall the weaver's speech. Throughout his writings
Stephens is concerned with social injustice, and from the earliest
essays in *Sinn Féin* to the stories in *Etched in Moonlight* this
topic may be traced.

Upon hearing the traditional names for Ireland, the young
man is deeply moved:

> He yearned to do deeds of valour, violent, grandiose feats
> which would redound to [Ireland's] credit and make the
> name of Irishmen synonymous with either greatness or singu-
> larity: for, as yet, the distinction between these words was
> no more clear to him than it is to any other young man
> who reads violence as heroism and eccentricity as genius.[16]

Like Mary, he can view the world in romantic, folkloric terms;
he sees England as an ogre, Ireland as a distressed, proud
queen. In *The Crock of Gold*, Caitilin Ni Murrachu chooses
Angus Óg, the god who loves his people, over Pan, the Hellenic
god of the sensual passions. Although the action in *The Charwoman's Daughter* is comic, Mary's preference for the lodger is
a decision for both patriotic and humanitarian concern for
others over materialistic and selfish emotions.

It is clear from Stephens' first draft of *The Charwoman's
Daughter* that he originally intended to end his story with the
lodger's recitation of his battle with the Policeman, and the
author's benevolent remarks on bruises and his affectionate
farewell to Mary Makebelieve.[17] It was after he had written
this farewell and the words, "The End," that Stephens added
the material found in Chapter XXXII, that is, the fairy-tale
ending with the providential death of a wealthy uncle and
the more realistic material in which the narrator explains why
the young man has an ally in poverty.

Although this new chapter is an abrupt shift in tone and
content, its aphoristic lines point ahead to Stephens' next works
of fiction. His commentary on the dullness of the golden mean
puts forth the thesis that "it is contrary to the laws of life
to possess that which other people do not want; therefore,
your beer shall foam, your wife shall be pretty, and your little
truth shall have a plum in it."[18] This thought is reiterated
in his short story, "The Triangle":

There is no satisfaction in owning that which nobody else covets. Our silver is no more than second-hand, tarnished metal until some one else speaks of it in terms of envy. Our husbands are barely tolerable until a lady friend has endeavoured to abstract their cloying attentions. Then only do we comprehend that our possessions are unique, beautiful, well worth guarding.[19]

Another idea drawn from Blake, that by the interaction of good and evil all things are possible, will be a major theme in *The Demi-Gods*. A defense of hunger as opposed to satiety which Stephens calls "all those negatives which culminate in greediness, stupidity, and decay" looks forward to Pan's contention in *The Crock of Gold* that hunger is the "greatest thing in the world."[20] By including this chapter, Stephens was also able to provide an ending in keeping with the genre with which he began. The aspects of the *Märchen* are satisfied: the poor but good Makebelieves end in riches and happiness.

THE CROCK OF GOLD (1912)

Stephens started to prepare himself for the writing of his second novel in 1909. From a beginning of ideas taken from contributions to *Sinn Féin* — political essays, sketches centered around the Old Philosopher, and short stories — the novel grew steadily, becoming more comprehensive in content and technique than his first work of fiction. *The Charwoman's Daughter* begins in the style of the *Märchen*, then becomes realistic and later aphoristic. In *The Crock of Gold* Stephens works these styles more closely together so that the account of Caitilin Ni Murrachu's union with Angus Óg is at once a fairy tale, a love story, and an object lesson.

This book is deliberately Irish in characterization, setting, and theme, but less stridently patriotic than the *Sinn Féin* essays which preceded it. Angus Óg is not one of the Gaelic warriors such as Finn or Cúchulinn; rather he is the god of poetry, of love, of divine imagination. His setting is the forest, his followers are those who seek inspiration not revenge. His combat with Pan is philosophical in nature, his victory spiritual despite the physicality represented in Caitilin's naked body. Angus Óg's victory would not be what Arthur Griffith and his political compatriots envisioned; it comes closer to the belief of AE, Yeats, and others in old gods who inspire and teach the Irish people. Stephens will deal with the bloody battles of the Irish saga in later novels; here he celebrates the triumph of charity and creativity.

The relationship between the Philosopher and the Thin Woman in this novel also grows out of material published in *Sinn Féin*, in the form of lectures given by an old curmudgeon to a not-always-willing listener. But the battles of husband and wife serve thematic aspects of the novel as well as providing comic relief. The Philosopher talks incessantly, giving forth information on every subject imaginable, but reacting to nothing; his wife rages and snaps, allowing her feelings to show but hugging to herself secrets about life. He is all mind, she all emotion. They remain nameless, unlike the other characters including their children, because they are components of one person. Like Jack Sprat and his wife, they are eminently suited to each other's needs, and when they finally discover this, they are joined in a true marriage of the Contraries.

When the characters in this novel interact, the theme of *The Crock of Gold* emerges: charity triumphs over selfishness, materialism, and lust. Angus Óg is the catalyst: before they meet him, the Philosopher and his wife pursue individual rather than collective goals; Caitilin seeks bodily comfort with Pan; Meehawl and the leprecauns concern themselves solely with possessions; while the policemen follow the rules without regard for human rights. Angus changes the lives of these people, teaching them, in plain words, that love conquers all.

The Crock of Gold is a fantasy, the transformation of the impossible into a condition of "fact," a game played by both author and reader for the purpose of entertainment, diversion, and subtle commentary on the world. The commentary in this case is on Irish nationalism, the psychology of human relations, and the stultifying aspects of religion, the law, and state-hood, among other things. It is also a sometimes serious, some-times irreverent view of the Literary Revival and its parapher-nalia of gods, avatars, and mystical rituals. Further, it contains philosophical debates, slapstick comedy, a romance between a mortal and a god, and the life stories of two prisoners. Its characters range from the mundane (shepherds) to the magnifi-cent (Celtic gods), its settings from an enchanted mountain to a village jail. Stephens' success in combining these divergent elements into a cohesive novel is an example of his literary craftsmanship.[21]

This is a tale told by a bemused story-teller given on occasion to asides but generally content to launch his characters and then let them find their destiny. His story begins with two seemingly unrelated acts, the "suicides" of a philosopher and his wife and the robbery of a pot of gold, and yet the remaining action of the plot is dependent upon these events. Moreover, the comment of the second philosopher upon hearing that his colleague proposes to die is anticipatory of the novel's close: "the ultimate end" is gaiety, music, and a dance of joy. The robbery also looks forward to the end of the story in which the crock of gold, an imprisoned philosopher, and a lost shepherdess are returned to their rightful places.

The deaths are the inevitable conclusion of the lives of dissatisfied people. The two philosophers are characterized in the first chapter of the book as men unable to deal with quite commonplace events. The birth of their children confounds the men; they are "forced to admire an event which they had been unable to prognosticate." The sound of birds singing annoys them; they are violently opposed to "noise." By these wry asides, Stephens demonstrates the philosophers' lack of emotion and their inability to appreciate life's natural forces. In his treatment of their wives, the author employs the same gentle irony to emphasize their irrational nature. He explains that each woman hated her own child but loved the other's baby, and solemnly reports that the women resolved this dilemma by swapping children.

The philosophers are not totally alike, however; the second man is capable of doubt concerning the value of a life built upon the pursuit of wisdom alone. But he is as yet lacking in the qualities which Stephens places beyond wisdom — goodness and kindness. Although capable of wondering whether the end of life might not be gaiety, the Philosopher has not progressed beyond the point where he can calmly state that he wishes to discuss his friend's resolution to commit suicide not in order to attempt to change his mind but "merely to continue an interesting conversation." The conversation does not alter his companion's decision. The other philosopher proceeds to extinguish his life by spinning like a religious dervish, and he is joined in this unique method of self-annihilation by his wife.

In contrast to this serious note, the next two chapters furnish comic relief in the form of the Philosopher's rambling discourses on the theoretical aspects of washing and sleep. These lectures, which are constantly being interrupted by the Philosopher's audiences, are accompanied by the narrator's waggish comments, for example, this aphorism: "A Leprecaun without a pot of gold is like a rose without perfume, a bird without a wing, or an inside without an outside."[22]

The Philosopher's lecture on washing is the result of the arrival of his neighbor, Meehawl Mac Murrachu, who twice comes to the cottage in the woods seeking advice concerning lost items: a washing-board and a daughter. He is given directions by the Philosopher which lead, in the first case, to the leprecauns' pot of gold. The second item is a more difficult problem for the Philosopher to solve.

Caitilin Ni Murrachu, "the most beautiful girl in the world," is not described in any detailed manner: the reader does not learn the color of her eyes or hair or skin. Her beauty of body and spirit must be assumed on the basis of the reactions of Pan, Angus Óg, the Philosopher, and his children to her. Her name recalls Caitilin ni Houlihan, a common name for Ireland. Her disappearance, then, is a matter of concern; indeed, it requires divine assistance to bring the girl back to her people. In contrast, another disappearance, the kidnapping of the Philosopher's children, is a humorous event which affords Stephens an opportunity to describe the life style of leprecauns.

When the children, who have been released by the leprecauns, are sent by their father as envoys to Pan's cave, they fail to convince Caitilin to return to her family. The Philosopher then undertakes the assignment. Unsuccessful as his children, he leaves the cave after engaging in a short debate with Pan over the meaning of the concept of virtue; he must seek a higher authority's aid, the Celtic god of love Angus Óg. Although he has objected to Pan's characterization of wisdom as a "catalogue of sensual stimuli," the Philosopher, while setting out on his journey, recalls Caitilin in her naked beauty. He sees the sunny landscape, he takes pleasure in the heat of the sun, he enjoys his food, and he indulges in a frivolous conversation ending in an impetuous kiss. To his surprise, he realizes that he finds luxuriating in the senses a pleasant change from constant thinking. However, he is not yet able to understand emotions: he infuriates the woman he has kissed by offering to apologize to her husband; his response to the tears of a homeless old woman is embarrassed silence; he must flee from a tinker woman who insists that she wants to marry him.[23]

The Philosopher's visit to Pan and Caitilin provokes an argument over virtue. His appeal to Angus Óg results in a debate in which Angus and Pan examine the question of what constitutes "the greatest thing in the world." The debate between the two gods is important because Caitilin, who represents Ireland, chooses divine imagination, championed by the Irish god, over hunger, represented by the Greek one. Thus Stephens suggests that Ireland must choose national literature and culture over the materialism of outside influences.

This point, the victory of Irish forces of spiritual life over the baser material desires, is emphasized in the Philosopher's adventures on his way home. His visit has transformed him into a charitable, responsive person. Although he is very hungry, he shares his cake with seven strangers, a greater sacrifice than his gift to the married woman of extra, unwanted food. Upon meeting an unhappy girl, he spontaneously offers assistance; this willingness to counsel is in contrast to his earlier escape from the old woman's tearful complaints. His discussion with young Mac Cushin is a delightful and serious conversation, as opposed to the exchange of arguments and misunderstandings which mar his visit with the tinkers.

While returning home, the Philosopher delivers three messages from Angus, and the messages and the strangers to whom they are directed are further indications of Stephens' espousal of the aims of the Irish Literary Revival. The strangers are called Mac Cúl, Mac Culain, and Mac Cushin. The names are variations of Cool (Cumhail), Cúchulinn, and Usheen (Oisín). Since the prefix Mac means "son of," the men are to be viewed in much the way that Stephens and his literary contemporaries viewed all Irishmen — as heirs of the ancient Gaelic heroes. Mac Cúl and Mac Culain, the "sons" of the famous Irish warriors, Cumhail[24] and Cúchulinn, respond to their messages in their hearts, but only Mac Cushin, a descendant of Oisín, the great poet of the Gaels, is able to fully understand and act on the directive to awaken the people of Ireland.

The Philosopher's new-found happiness is abruptly interrupted when, on reaching his home, he is arrested on charges
of having murdered his colleague and the colleague's wife.
The leprecauns, still angered over their lost gold, have turned
informers and sent information to the police concerning bodies
buried under a hearthstone. The narration of the march to
the village police station is punctuated with goofy verbal contests
between the Philosopher and his dim-witted captors, but the
period which follows, in which the Philosopher resides in jail
awaiting trial and execution, is somber.

Included in the novel at this point are two stories by Stephens
which first appeared in *Sinn Féin* in 1909. These stories have
been reworked for use as tales told by the Philosopher's fellow
prisoners, but they have still earned some critical attack on
the grounds that they are irrelevant to the main plot of the
novel.[25] It is true that they are not essential to the novel,
but it is also true that they serve a purpose. Both stories concern
clerks who have lost their jobs because of illness or old age
and who, because of the economic structure which Mrs. Makebelieve and the young lodger have condemned in *The Charwoman's
Daughter*, are unable to make a living honestly. Stephens' point,
also made in "Builders," an essay printed in *Sinn Féin* in 1907,
and to be made again in "Hunger," a short story he published
in 1918, is that a healthy society is one in which men do
not starve to death or face imprisonment when their age prevents
them from working. Victims of an industrialized society, the
aged and the infirm are as much in need of the humanitarianism
of Angus Óg as the Philosopher, the Thin Woman, and Caitilin
Ni Murrachu.

In Book VI of the novel, the children discover and hand
over the crock of gold to the leprecauns, and they accompany
their mother on her journey to request the aid of Angus Óg.
The journey of the Thin Woman is, like that of her husband,
one of meetings with strangers; among these are the symbolic
characters, the Absolutes, who block the Thin Woman's passage
until she can successfully argue her way clear of them. The
Thin Woman also attempts to instruct her children in the
area of eternal strife between men and women. To counter-
balance these serious narrative passages, Stephens inserts comedy: a light hearted discussion on why cows say "moo" and

an animated conversation between a cow and a fly.

At the Thin Woman's request, Angus Óg summons his people, and he and the fairy host march to the city to release the Philosopher and others from prison; they then return to the countryside. Thus, order and harmony are restored. The gaiety, the music, and the dance of joy envisioned by the Philosopher at the beginning of the book form the background for the ending. Moreover, the dancer's circular pattern, from countryside to city to a return to the home of the gods, is both descriptive of the plot and, Stephens hopes, prophetic of Ireland's future. *The Crock of Gold* is concerned with a descent into corrupt civilization and a return to beneficial nature. Ireland in the form of Caitilin, must make her way from Pan to Angus, from foreign to Gaelic gods, from base materialism to divine spirituality.

The Crock of Gold is, among other things, a prophecy and as such it is not surprising that Stephens, in writing the book, paid reverence to William Blake. During this period in Stephens' career, Blake was his mentor, as he was for W. B. Yeats, AE, and other writers of the Literary Revival.[26] Stephens often acknowledged this influence on his artistic career. He admitted in 1914 that he was producing "Blakeish" poems; certainly many of his poetic works before and after that date could be similarly termed.[27] Stephens' fiction in this period also reveals his literary indebtedness. In *The Charwoman's Daughter*, Stephens' remark that all things are possible "by the interaction perhaps cooperation" of good and evil, his defense in that work of hunger as a better condition than satiety, and his belief, in *The Crock of Gold*, that there is no "fertility" unless extremes meet are all related to Blake's dictum: "without Contraries is no progression."[28] Characters in his later fiction also serve to demonstrate this proposition. In his third novel, two demi-gods, Finaun and Caeltia, represent the strife between knowledge and emotion. Appropriately enough, their human counterparts, Eileen and Patsy, are also in conflict throughout the novel. The battle of the opposites in *Deirdre* is between Conachúr, representing conservative old age, and Naoise, representing rebellious youth. Ideas expressed in Stephens' early essays also reflect Blake's concept of the Contraries. In "Tattered Thoughts" he holds that "if everyone was virtuous vice would be a distinction," and in "Irish Idiosyncrasies" he says that "good and evil are energies working in opposite directions."[29] Stephens does not acknowledge the source of his ideas in these essays, but in a later article he admits that he finds Blake "very good to steal from; and let it be conceded that theft is the first duty of man."[30] In another article, he lauds his precursor as "the sole example we have of the myth maker not only in modern, but even in historical literature."[31]

Throughout his writings, Stephens, with Blake, condemns the tyranny of misguided authority, the hypocrisy of organized religion, and the materialism and exploitation to be found in industrialized society. His conception of Angus Óg's mission seems to be taken from the epigraph chosen by Blake for "The Four Zoas": "For we wrestle not against flesh and blood, but against principalities, against powers, against the rulers of the darkness of this world, against spiritual wickedness in high places." In *The Demi-Gods* he looks forward to a Jerusalem in Ireland ". . . we scatter our sins broadcast and call them our neighbours'; let us scatter our virtues abroad and build us a city to live in."[32]

Stephens characterizes Blake as "the man who wrote the best epigrams of our language."[33] In *The Crock of Gold* he attempts to reproduce Blake's epigrams in the maxims attributed to the philosophers and their wives. The women's belief that "man is God's secret, Power is man's secret, Sex is woman's secret" is a line which recalls the style and thought of "The Proverbs of Hell."[34] A discussion in the novel of "divinely erratic energy" concludes with Blake's explanation that "the crooked roads are the roads of genius."[35] Stephens uses this maxim again in "An Essay in Cubes" to support his claim that Blake is the only writer who could be called a genius.[36] Many passages in the novel resemble Blake's writing, for example, these two selections:

> The finger-tips are guided by God, but the devil looks through the eyes of all creatures so that they may wander in the errors of reason and justify themselves of their wanderings.[37]

> Statecraft, also, that tender Shepherd of the Flocks, has been despoiled of his crook and bell, and wanders in unknown desolation while, beneath the banner of Politics, Reason sits howling over an intellectual chaos.[38]

In a book review published in the same year as *The Crock of Gold*, Stephens remarks that the recurrent theme in Blake's mystical works is the interaction of the Four Zoas and their struggles for domination over each other which end when "Imagination, or The Redeemer, has fused them into the peace of Universal Brotherhood."[39] Stephens works with this same theme in his novel. The antagonisms of the Zoas — Urizen (reason), Luvah (passion), Tharmas (body, the senses), Urthona (spirit, divine imagination) — are illustrated in two conflicts, the quarrels between the Philosopher and the Thin Woman and the opposing theories of Pan and Angus Óg.

His reliance upon intellect has brought the Philosopher to a state in which he, like Urizen, has cast aside pleasure. The Thin Woman, who lost her stores of knowledge and who walks in "the valleys of anger," has reached the point where she, like Luvah or his female fragmentation Vala, is governed by emotion without the guidance of thought. Pan is Stephens' Tharmas: he advocates a sterile and destructive concentration upon the senses, those qualities Angus Óg lists as "Desire and Fever and Lust and Death." He awakens Caitilin to an awareness of sensual pleasures, but their relationship is incomplete because she represents Enitharmon, whose true mate is Los, or Angus Óg. When Angus is in union with Caitilin, he is Urthona, and his people are Urthona's "Gods of the Heathen." In his company, Caitilin, the Philosopher, and the Thin Woman can be transported beyond Beulah; they can gain a "sense of oneness."

The Three Absolutes encountered by the Thin Woman are "The Ancient Britons" about whom Blake writes:

In the last Battle of King Arthur only Three Britons escaped, these were the Strongest Man, the Beautifullest Man, and the Ugliest Man; these three marched through the field unsubdued, as Gods, and the Sun of Britain [set], but shall rise again with tenfold splendor when Arthur shall awake from sleep, and resume his dominion over earth and ocean.[40]

Blake's Britons become Irish figures in *The Crock of Gold*, awaiting Angus Óg, the Celtic god of Imagination, and his son, the Redeemer who will be born of the god's union with Caitilin Ni Murrachu. Blake designated his Beautiful Man as the human pathetic, his Strong Man as the human sublime, and his Ugly Man as the human reason. Stephens' Absolutes are Thought, Love, and Generation — representations of the qualities found in the Philosopher, the Thin Woman, and Pan.

Stephens' admiration of Blake took the form of adaption of Blake's style, characters, and beliefs. In *The Crock of Gold* there are three themes which Stephens found in Blake's writings and made his own: the enmity between men and women, the happy innocence of childhood, and the need to embrace life's joys and its responsibilities.

Book VI opens with the comment that the Thin Woman's ability to be angry is unlimited. At the beginning of the novel, the Philosopher and his colleague learn that their wives' anger is "more valuable than the friendship of angels" because in their state of irritation the women repeat the fourteen hundred maledictions which make up their knowledge, thus increasing their husbands' wisdom. The Thin Woman's anger is intensified when the leprecauns report to her that their pot of gold has been stolen by Meehawl Mac Murrachu while he is operating under the Philosopher's directions for the location of a lost washing-board. She announces emphatically that all her sympathies are with the leprecauns of Gort na Cloca Mora.

The quarrels between the Thin Woman and the Philosopher are illustrative of female Emotion in perpetual battle with male Thought. In his poem, "Mount Derision," Stephens pictures Heart and Thought as chained to each other like Blake's Oothoon and Theotormon. In this work, the torture is verbal rather than physical, and the chains are marital. The disagreements between the philosophers and their wives are exemplified in their maxims: the women believe in storage of knowledge and secrecy; their husbands wish to offer others their knowledge because they believe that "refilling is progress."

Stephens, like Blake, views this conflict as universal but not irreversible. Indeed, spiritual transformation is brought about by enmity. When the children return from their unsuccessful mission to Pan's cave, the Philosopher asks his wife to undertake an assignment as his messenger. She indignantly refuses, and he is forced to set out himself for the stronghold of Angus Óg. Because of this errand, he receives the instruction of the Celtic god in whom Thought and Emotion are united, and he is inspired to love humanity.

The Thin Woman's response to the Philosopher's new tenderness is stunned silence, then a recovery to make his favorite food, to weep, and to proclaim her husband's beauty and goodness. Conflict between the sexes has ended, but the female also must go through certain initiation rites. Having previously refused to undertake a journey on the grounds that it would be an impropriety for a lady to leave her household, she must now travel the countryside at night in order to find Angus Óg; and before setting out, she must take part in "that sacrifice which is called Forgiveness of Enemies." Thus, Stephens echoes Blake's axiom: "Without Forgiveness of Sin, Love is Itself Eternal Death."

With the cessation of adult enmity, child-like innocence may return, for Stephens believes that the "knowledge of a man is added to the gaiety of a child."[41] Stephens' children behave instinctively. Seumas and Brigid Beg do not think out their reactions, they react; and although their actions are unpremeditated, they are wise because they bring happiness into the world. The culmination of this instinctual wisdom is the children's return of the leprecauns' gold, but its beginnings are found much earlier in the story.

Unlike the adults who live in the darkness of the forest, Seumas and his sister choose to play in the sunlight. It is the little boy who discovers a patch of sunshine, and Stephens praises his namesake's curiosity as one of the "great impelling forces of life." Seumas and Brigid Beg also play happily and freely with the creatures in the forest. The children are not only able to recognize differences in the birds' personalities, but they are able to understand a cow's emotions.[42] With equal spontaneity and attention they listen to the leprecauns and Pan, and their responses are honest and frequently quite perceptive. They explain when questioned that they do not know if they like their father and that the most memorable thing about their mother is that she pinches them. After parting from a leprecaun, Brigid admits that she likes him even when he is not in a good humor, a view with which her brother concurs; a little later, Seumas excuses Pan's strained manner on the grounds of his being "sick."

Two other young people, Tomás and Mac Cushin, share the children's natural relationships with all living creatures. Tomás loves dogs and horses to the point of his mother's distraction, but when he learns that the policemen intend to hang the Philosopher, he demonstrates his concern for human beings by attacking the officers. Mac Cushin instructs the Philosopher on the subject of youth, and he is the only stranger who is able to interpret the words of Angus Óg. It is significant that the three to whom Angus sends messages are progressively younger in age and that the youngest man receives the most important news, that he is going to write a poem which will rouse the slumbering Irish people.

Caitilin Ni Murrachu occupies the middle ground between childhood and maturity, her age being representative of Ireland on the threshold of cultural awakening. When she is first seen, the shepherdess and her animals are dancing to Pan's music. Seumas and Brigid Beg also dance and sing as they follow the path to Pan's cave, and their father moves ecstatically in the sunlight when he leaves the god's dwelling.

But Pan's music, while it extols the senses, celebrates only the depths of the passions. He tells Caitilin that right and wrong are merely words, that the creatures of nature are part of an unthinking cycle of existence. Caitilin's happiness in her sexual freedom is marred by her dissatisfaction with this philosophy, although she does not know what further goals to seek. It is from Angus Óg that she learns of a happiness built upon both physical and spiritual love, because in this god, passion, intellect, and the senses are combined through imagination. He helps her to develop a concern for others; she learns "to renounce the little ego that the mighty ego may have life."

However different in age and temperament, the mortals who are influenced by the Celtic god share one quality, an enjoyment of the art of dancing. This might seem at first to be a negligible accomplishment, but Stephens holds it to be one of the highest possible achievements because it is representative of a joyous acceptance of life.[43] According to him, a leprecaun is more valuable than a Prime Minister because he is able to dance and make merry. When the Philosopher is rescued from his police escort by the leprecauns, he says that he is tempted to stay with them because he has learned that dancing is man's "first and last duty."

In the second chapter of the book, the Philosopher asks his colleague whether he can dance with a woman of the *Shi* (fairy fort). His associate rejects this prospect just as he has rejected most of life's possibilities. The pursuit of wisdom has quite literally bored him to death. The dance which the Philosopher has proposed would have been a moonlight activity; as the Thin Woman explains to her children, the fairies dance at night because "self-righteous moralities" have driven the creatures of Druidism from the world during the day.

Until the end of the novel Angus Óg cannot dance because of his sadness over the world of evil and unhappiness in which his people must live. It is appropriate, then, that the novel ends with a dance performed by the fairy host as they march in the sunlight to free man from worldly corruption. This final dance is Stephens' version of a fusion of the Zoas, for dance is the body calling forth its senses (Tharmas); it is the beauty of orderly patterns (Urizen); it is a response to love (Luvah); and it is a creation of the imagination (Urthona). Those who dance have attained Blake's fourfold vision.

Stephens loved to dance, moving to musical rhythm as Joyce did, in a strangely compelling way. That he would use a favorite pastime as a symbol leads to further consideration of what parts of the novel reveal its author's private life. Obviously the characters of Seumas Beg and the Philosopher suggest youthful and mature aspects of the author. Seumas and Brigid are also the vision of a fond father who has endowed them with the most admirable characteristics: curiosity, honesty, animation, and good will. The Philosopher's piquant lines are vintage Stephens, but his habit of non-stop talking is AE's. Augustine Martin's view of the old gentleman in "There Is a Tavern in the Town" as a "tedious old cod" may be debatable, but he is correct in pointing out his reincarnation as the "irresistible old cod" of *The Crock of Gold*. Martin explains, "this must be one of the few instances in literature where the dialogue of a character was written before the character himself had been called into existence."[44] On the contrary, this appears to be an example in which the character had to be invented because he already existed — in the person of AE. Cynthia Stephens also served as a model, for Caitilin's beauty and love of the outdoors recalls Stephens' wife, an extraordinarily lovely and accomplished horsewoman.

But more than a revelation of aspects of the author's life, the novel is a demonstration of his art. If it can be argued that Yeats strove to perfect his life rather than his work, Stephens chose the reverse course. However, despite general agreement among critics that *The Crock of Gold* is one of the best, if not the best of his works, little note has been taken of the fact that, like many other masterworks of literature, *The Crock of Gold* was not achieved without compositional struggle. The first draft of the novel, written on the recto pages of six stenographic notebooks, is instructive. The presence of over three thousand revisions on these pages indicates that Stephens was closely attending to his story; but beyond these corrections, certain aspects of the work required further rewriting. This was accomplished by adding new material on the verso pages of the notebooks.

There are 132 such additions to the manuscript; they vary in length and significance, but the majority of them reveal Stephens at work on the clarification and integration of his materials. Many contribute to the structure, characterization, and tone: the inclusion of wry remarks about the philosophers' opposition to noise and their wives' proposal to swap children; Meehawl's interruptions of the Philosopher's rambling lectures, sections filled with a manic glee; extensive revisions of the debate between Angus Óg and Pan and the narrator's commentary in Chapter XIII on politics and justice; expansions of the ludicrous verbal contest between the Philosopher and his dull-witted captors; additions of epigrams and maxims to demonstrate the beliefs of the characters; further notations of the development of thought processes; and expansion of the section in which the Thin Woman encounters the Three Absolutes.

The additions show the author in the moment of composition, blending characterization and action, serious debate and comic relief, fantasy and reality. Some of the added material was "stolen" from Blake, but one suspects that the English poet would have approved of the energy, grace, and appreciation with which Stephens adapted his ideas and style.

At the beginning of this section a reference was made to Stephens' "literary craftsmanship." How is this manifested? Using *The Crock of Gold* as a case study, it consists of Stephens' ability to make critical judgments: where to insert comic relief, where to balance lengthy exposition with humorous one-liners, how to draw upon Blakean ideas, Irish mythology, and Eastern thought, how to select what is appropriate to the work so that it is not overloaded with allusions. Stephens weaves material used elsewhere so well that it becomes a necessary part of his new fabric. He presents characters at first only briefly sketched but so richly diverse in their actions and thoughts that they change the reader's view of the world and of human nature. He uses a language which is clear, apt, and lyrical, and he combines childlike wonder at magical events with the adult's understanding of the ways of the heart.

THE DEMI-GODS (1914)

In *The Demi-Gods* Stephens relates the adventures of three angels and their hosts, Patsy Mac Cann, a tinker, and his daughter Mary. Finaun is a wise, kindly Archangel who serves as a spiritual guardian for Eileen Ni Cooley, a worldly, hot-tempered woman who walks the countryside seeking adventures. Caeltia, a Seraph, is a dark-haired, determined guardian for Patsy, a man whom he closely resembles. Art, a handsome Cherub who is described as not yet having fulfilled a "high destiny," is not assigned a guardianship although he is clearly identified in his youthful beauty with Mary Mac Cann. Cuchulain, a fourth demi-god, is a young Seraph who, like Arcade, the anarchist in Anatole France's *La Révolte des Anges*, is remarkable for his celestial beauty and his unangelic rebelliousness.[45] He is connected with Billy the Music, an itinerant concertina player encountered by the others in their travels.

Two poems printed in 1911 and 1912 are starting points for the novel.[46] The first, "In the Poppy Field," introduces Mad Patsy, a man who refuses to work for "any clown"; in *The Demi-Gods*, Patsy Mac Cann talks about a "great friend" who refuses to work for anyone, and he explains that he also does not work if he can help it. In the second poem, "Mac Dhoul," the protagonist, seeing the heavenly throne empty for a moment, hops on it, and for his impudence gets flipped back to earth as unceremoniously as Cuchulain and Brien O'Brien are in the story told in the novel by Caeltia.

Stephens' story of gods and men may also be linked to his later poem, "Envying Tobias," which begins:

No more do we
Of angels talk:
'Tis no more of any read,

That an angel came
With us to walk,
And to a woman said

— Blessed be thou,
To thee I bow
My wise and lovely head —[47]

The story of Tobit is the tale of a deeply religious man who is subjected to the tests of blindness, poverty, and his wife's desertion. The angel Raphael is sent in the guise of a beautiful man who offers to accompany Tobit's son as a servant when he goes on the road to another city to obtain money for his father. The angel leads the boy safely to his destination, offers him good advice, and dispatches a devil tormenting Sara, a young woman, so that the boy may marry her. The story, probably written as early as 200 and 250 BC, is demonstrative of the ancient virtues of loyalty to parents, respectful burial of the dead, and the efficacy of prayer.

Patsy Mac Cann, like Tobit, feeds the hungry and clothes the naked (the demi-gods as well as himself) and is careful to bury the dead (Brien O'Brien). Stephens' three demi-gods represent Raphael's qualities: practical judgment (Caeltia), imposing wisdom (Finaun), and physical beauty and youth (Art). Tobit and Sara are treated more severely than Patsy and Mary, but Stephens' characters pass the tests imposed upon them and are rewarded at the end. Tobit regains his eyesight, his wife, and his wealth; Patsy views life in a less mercenary fashion, he is rejoined by Eileen, and he gets to keep a small portion of the gold he has taken from the house of a rich man. Mary Mac Cann, like Sara, wins a husband.

In many ways, Stephens' third novel is not significantly different in structure from its predecessors. Symbolism and naturalism are compounded again in this story of angels who appear on earth to the bewilderment, delight, and occasional distress of a group who walk the Irish countryside. Demi-gods and tinkers converse and live together in a manner as happy as the relationships among the gods, fairies, leprecauns, and mortals in *The Crock of Gold*. The novel is narrated in the fashion of one who has lived on the road, just as *The Charwoman's Daughter* is a first-hand account of life among the poor people of Dublin. The demi-gods travel with their hosts southward from Donegal, through Connemara, on to Kerry, and then northward to Donegal again. It is a cyclical journey such as the procession of the gods at the end of the second novel, but the men and women whom they meet on the road are not symbolic figures; they are as realistic as their settings. Indeed, Stephens may have talked with people by the name of Mac Cann in a walk, in early years, to Belfast; several years after the novel's publication, Padraig Mac Gréine listed the family as tinkers in County Cavan.[48]

The first three novels by Stephens deal with a basic conflict, the struggle between a maturing daughter and a strong parent. Mary Makebelieve opposes her mother on a fairly minor level, by not telling her of her meetings with the Policeman and not returning home immediately one evening. Caitilin Ni Murrachu is more independent; she leaves home to live first with Pan and then with Angus Óg, and despite her father's "ambassadors," she does not return. In *The Demi-Gods*, Mary Mac Cann and her father quarrel openly and frequently, and she is not only able to hold her own in these arguments, but she is also able to influence the course of their actions. It is her decision that Mac Cann must recover the clothing he has stolen from the angels.

Perhaps because Stephens' young heroines are raised without companions of their own age, they are anxious to assume the role of mother. Mary Makebelieve talks to ducklings in an attempt to be affectionate, Caitilin "mothers" cows and goats, and Mary Mac Cann hugs her donkey. In her loneliness, Mary Makebelieve longs to shake a man's hand, and Caitilin's isolation is such that "the fingers of her soul stretched out to clasp a stranger's." Mary Mac Cann is happier than these two, because even as her story begins she is able to cook, wash, and care for four men.

Other portions of Stephens' second and third novels are also related. In *The Crock of Gold*, the woman who travels with two tinkers wants to leave her companions and go off with the Philosopher, an unwilling stranger. An equally forthright

woman, Eileen Ni Cooley, offers a similar plan to a disinterested
angel in *The Demi-Gods*. The tinker woman's belief that hunger
makes hares out of men is a view seconded by Billy the Music,
who calls his workers "sheep." When the Philosopher and
the tinkers are eating supper, a conversation takes place between
an ass and a spider which bears a distinct resemblance to
one between Art and a spider.

Three of the demi-gods are a reworking of the men who
speak to the Thin Woman in *The Crock of Gold*. In his portraits
of the Three Absolutes, Stephens equates beauty with thought,
strength with love, and ugliness with generation. In *The Demi-
Gods*, the most beautiful man, Art, represents love and generation; Finaun and Caeltia represent thought and strength;
there is no ugliest man. the demi-gods are also similar to those
characters in *The Crock of Gold* who receive Angus Óg's message,
Mac Cúl, Mac Culain, and Mac Cushin. Mac Cúl and Finaun
are old and kindly; Mac Culain and Caeltia are younger and
they are both quick-tongued; Mac Cushin and Art are youthful,
poetic, and easy-going.

In all three novels, Stephens explores some favorite topics:
the personality traits and behavior of animals, the tyrannies
of a materialistic society, the conflict between the sexes, and
certain Theosophical beliefs.

Stephens writes with obvious pleasure of the eels and ducklings
of St. Stephen's Green and the squirrels and rabbits of Coilla
Doraca, but in a BBC broadcast many years later, he acknowledged: "I am inclined to think that the three most beautiful
things in the world are: a goat, a donkey and a mountain.
I mean by that, any goat, any ass and any mountain."[49] Mac
Cann's donkey is not unlike the goat in *The Crock of Gold*.
Both animals are handsome and capable of rationality; the
latter quality is revealed by looking at their eyes. Mac Cann's
donkey peers at "the world without in order to focus steadily
the world within." Throughout *The Demi-Gods*, the bond
between man and nature is reciprocal — if donkeys and birds
may take on the mantle of rationality, then humans may draw
their traits from the lower animals. Thus, Mac Cann is now
a wolf or a vulture, now a sheep or a deer, while that paradoxical
creature, woman, is as economical as an ant and as extravagant
as a bee.

In *The Charwoman's Daughter*, Mrs. Makebelieve has been

Stephens' spokesman for his ideas on economics; in *The Demi-Gods*, Stephens uses Patsy as an exemplar. The difference between Patsy and the other men is that he lives outside of society, ducking its laws:

> ... he crawled under or vaulted across these ethical barriers, and they troubled him no more than as he had to bend or climb a little to avoid them — he discerned laws as something to be avoided, and it was thus he saw most things.[50]

This commentary recalls a section on the Dublin slum dwellers in Stephens' first novel:

> They could dodge under the fences of the law and climb the barbed wire of morality with equal impunity, and the utmost rigour of punishment had little terror for those whose hardships could scarcely be artificially worsened.[51]

In his third novel Stephens constructs a system in which geographic and socioeconomic movements are plotted on horizontal and vertical scales in order to illustrate the difference between the employee and the vagabond. The ordinary man has social or economic potential, that is, the chance to move up or down on the social scale, but his geographic or horizontal movements are severely limited. Patsy, who by choice has no upward or downward range on the social scale, has a peripatetic life which gives him almost unlimited horizontal freedom.

In the conversation between Billy the Music and Patsy, Stephens examines a relationship which has always interested him, the internalized battle between employer and employee. When Billy complains that he was as helpless among tradespeople as his workers were with him, his reaction to the economic machine is an anticipation of the employer's resignation in "The Boss" because he feels that he is leading the life of a donkey.

Stephens' political and psychological theories reveal themselves during the passages narrating Patsy's adventures while reclaiming the angels' belongings. The argument between a man and woman which Patsy overhears recalls the scene in which two stories are overheard by the Philosopher in *The Crock of Gold*. The argument between husband and wife is, like the stories heard by the Philosopher, an illustration of the emotional sterility of urban society; the stories in the two novels are clearly intended to set up unflattering contrasts of city life with the happy innocence of country folk. The stories in the novels are also linked to two of Stephens' contributions to *Sinn Féin*, "The Seoinin" and "Mrs. Maurice M'Quillan," in which city-dwelling Irishmen attempt to imitate the English establishment and in the process gain only "provincial," "vulgar" traditions. What differentiates the scene in *The Demi-Gods* from the others is its sophistication: the woman's ideas on her mother's behavior and motives are new to the author who always idealized maternity.

A lengthy description of Mary Mac Cann in Chapter XI leads Stephens, inevitably, to exposition. This time the beginning topic is beauty, but he goes on to women, their relationships with men and other women, and the female struggle for power. The passage is an extension of his remarks in his first novel concerning husbands and wives and the Thin Woman's lecture to Seumas and Brigid Beg in *The Crock of Gold*.

In *The Demi-Gods* Stephens records a belief which is distinctly Theosophical: ". . . death is sorrowful at first and for a long time, but afterwards the dead are contented and learn to shape themselves anew." According to another Theosophical belief, spirits may teach those who are receptive. The Philosopher learns much about life from Angus Óg, and in *The Demi-Gods* four mortals receive lessons from their Guardians. Billy the Music has already learned by Cuchulain's threats and actions that to lust for wealth is foolish; when he meets the others he has already responded to the lessons by leaving his gold behind. Patsy is also guided by Caeltia into realizing that ill-gotten money should be thrown away. Apparently, Caeltia speaks to Eileen Ni Cooley on the same subject after she sees Patsy toss gold pieces in the ditch. Eileen learns from Finaun's story that there is eternal conflict between man and woman and that a woman should give freely of herself. She first offers Patsy a portion of her food, but as the story ends she is willing to travel the roads with him. Mary Mac Cann gains independence by learning to care for herself and for others. The only mortal who does not profit is the one who will not learn — Brien O'Brien returns to Rhadamanthus having added to his karmic disability by his cruelty on earth. Patsy's gift of a threepenny-piece which he places in the dead man's fist is an act of charity, but as a repetition of an earlier gift, the coin signals the start of another round for O'Brien.

The mystical doctrine of flux — the mobility of planes of existence — is assumed in *The Crock of Gold* and made explicit in *The Demi-Gods*. Angus Óg and Art are "planet-angels," who, in the Theosophical system, unite with the daughters of men to create the marriage of spirit and nature. Finaun tells Eileen a version of the creation story which posits reincarnation, Caeltia's tale deals with Karma, and Art's story concerns the rounds of a soul. The influence of Eastern thought is also apparent in Art's characterization. Four conditions were posted by Buddha as necessary for the existence of being: ordinary material food, contact of the sensory organs with the external world, unconsciousness, and mental volition or will. Art undergoes all four conditions in the stated order. The first is satisfied by the meals he shares with the Mac Canns. The second is fulfilled by his travels on the road. The third takes place near the end of the story when he is seen on the grass, lost in thought after having kissed Mary's hand. The fourth condition, *cetana*, is the conclusion of the story, the determination to rip up his wings and to live on earth. The only point on which Stephens seems in utter disagreement with Theosophy is the satirical manner in which he treats magic. The magician tells Art that the audience surrounding a magician must be fools.

But *The Demi-Gods* is not a Theosophical document. It is a picaresque novel with a host of adventures and more than one rogue. Stephens' original title for the novel was "The Degredation of the Demi-Gods." If "Degredation" is present, it is only in the portrayal of Cuchulain. The angel who bears the name of the most chivalrous hero in the Irish sagas has been represented as a contentious young Seraph who is thrown out of heaven for stealing. Finaun, Caeltia, and Art are represented more sympathetically, their author's error in placing Finaun, an Archangel, in charge of Caeltia and Art, who are a Seraph and a Cherub, being forgivable, as William Tindall has pointed out, because "not malice surely, but innocence" accounts for the error in theology.[52]

Anatole France displays a better knowledge of the heavenly orders in a book frequently compared to *The Demi-Gods*, *La*

Révolte des Anges. In France's book Arcade and his fellow con-
spirator, Zita, are lower-order angels of the third hierarchy,
while Istar, who is a seditious Cherub, takes the earthly title
of Prince to indicate that he is of the first order. Anatole
France's interpretation of a Cherub differs radically from that
of Stephens: Istar is a bull-like man who is capable of earthly
indulgences in love, unlike Stephens' Cherub, Art, who has
not "lived" yet. France's Archangel, Mirar, is a mild, henpecked
lover in contrast to the dignified old Finaun. Another character,
Nectaire, is more like Finaun in terms of his wisdom and
position of respect among the other angels; but Nectaire is
suitably designated as a Domination, one of the upper hierarchy.
Finally, unlike Stephens' angels who are dependent upon their
Irish friends for knowledge of food, Arcade and the others
adapt at once to the idea of eating. Their author, using as
examples the angels who visited Abraham and Lot, explains
that "les anges, sous l'aiguillon de la faim, mangent ainsi que
les animaux terrestres, et leur nourriture, transformée par la
chaleur digestive, s'identifie à leur céleste substance."[53]

The Demi-Gods is not, moreover, only an extension of Stephens'
first two novels. Its characters are new creations who afford
Stephens an opportunity to demonstrate his increasing ability
to capture speech and gesture humorously and effectively.
Stephens is bolder in his characterizations here, and he achieves
his descriptions in a less didactic fashion than before. He has
learned to sketch a character succinctly

> They set their camp among roaring fairs where every kind
> of wild man and woman yelled salutation at Patsy and his
> daughter, and howled remembrance of ten and twenty-year-
> old follies, and plunged into drink with the savage alacrity
> of those to whom despair is a fairer brother than hope . . . .

> Billy the Music did put another pinch of tobacco into his
> pipe, and after drawing on it meditatively for a few minutes
> he snuffed it out with his thumb and put it into his pocket.
> Naturally he put it in upside down, so that the tobacco
> might drop from the pipe, for he was no longer a saving
> man.

> Sometimes at night a ballad-singer would stray on their road,

an angry man from whom no person had purchased songs for two days, and in return for victual this one would entertain them with his lays and recite the curses he had composed against those who did not pay the musician.[54]

The book also contains far more dialogue than the first novel in which we find synopses of discussions among the characters, or the second in which the conversations mainly take the form of debates or lectures. In *The Demi-Gods*, Mac Cann and his daughter not only listen to tales but they talk to each other, to their angelic companions, and to their acquaintances. When Stephens decides to throw objectivity aside and to appear in the enthusiastic first-person, the results are not always as fortunate. A case in point is a passage in Chapter X in which the reader is assured that the stars watch over the Mac Canns' donkey with paternal concern:

What did they say to him? Down the glittering slopes they peer and nod; before his eyes the mighty pageant is unrolled in quiet splendour; for him too the signs are set. Does the Waterman care nothing for his thirst? Does the Ram not bless his increase? Against his enemies also the Archer will bend his azure bow and loose his arrows of burning gold.[55]

This relationship between ass and astrology is pretty silly.

While the first novel centers around visual images and the second appeals to both the visual and auditory senses, the third encompasses all the senses. So, too, the setting expands as Stephens progresses from one work to another. *The Charwoman's Daughter* is bordered by the city limits of Dublin. While *The Crock of Gold* encompasses both city and nearby countryside, *The Demi-Gods* covers an even larger section of Ireland. But, however original and bold Stephens has been in *The Demi-Gods*, when he created the ending of his third novel, he looked back on his earlier works of fiction. *The Demi-Gods* closes with the attainment of goals which we find in *The Crock of Gold* and *The Charwoman's Daughter*: the unions of man and woman, of gods and men, and of fantasy and reality.

Stephens was sufficiently fond of his story of angels and tinkers to rewrite it in another medium, drama, a treatment he did not accord his first two novels.[56] Hilary Pyle claims that *The Demi-Gods* was written first as a play.[57] Although the manuscript of the play is not dated, the draft is written on paper that provides evidence that it is later than the novel upon which it is based, and a typescript of the draft is dated August 1921.[58] Furthermore, several of the characters' speeches in the play have been written as they appear in the novel and then shortened, corrected, or rewritten. Only one of the five stories told in the novel, Finaun's story, remains in the play, and it has been drastically shortened and rearranged. The descriptive and narrative sections of a book obviously could not be included in the play, but Stephens manages to incorporate some of the material in his extensive stage directions.

The dialogue throughout the play is similar to the novel, but at the end when Art tears off his wings, he says: "You and I will go down after your people," and they exit together. The change from "the people" to "your people" better suggests the symbolic ending which Stephens had in mind for *The Demi-Gods*. The closing scene is certainly another version of the ending of *The Crock of Gold* in which Angus Óg goes down with Caitilin to her people. Both closings are representations of the aim of the Irish Literary Revival, to wed creativity with natural beauty in an effort to revitalize Ireland.

Why was the dramatic version of *The Demi-Gods* never performed or published? It is difficult to know. One possible reason is that critical reaction to the novel was disappointing to its author. Stephens wrote Warren Barton Blake: "I was glad to hear from you & particularly glad to know that you preferred my Demi-Gods to the Crock of Gold. We are in a minority of three. AE and you & myself are agreed on this point, but the vast majority of reviewers think otherwise & will continue to do so for some time."[59]

There were others who praised the book. Yeats wrote to Olivia Shakespear that of those he viewed as Stephens' "three best books," *The Demi-Gods*, *The Crock of Gold*, and *In the Land of Youth*, he preferred *The Demi-Gods*.[60] Thomas Bodkin liked the book, which relieved Stephens' mind considerably, since it was dedicated to Bodkin. Ernest Boyd joined the "minority" by declaring that he found *The Demi-Gods* a more mature and more controlled novel than *The Crock of Gold*.[61] This statement was in agreement with those made by Stephens in which he claimed that *The Demi-Gods* was "certainly much better written

& organized than the other [*The Crock of Gold*]," and that the novel was the "best written" of his first three.[62] But Stephens' gloomy prognosis proved correct. The book never received the critical attention and praise given to *The Crock of Gold*.[63] It is not surprising, then, that in the next works of fiction, he set out in a new direction.

3 The Quest That Destiny Commands

In an unpublished typescript entitled, "The Unity of National Culture in Ireland," Stephens appeals to his countrymen and, more specifically, to his literary compatriots to maintain a separate culture from that of England.[1] At first glance there is nothing odd about such an appeal — it is reflective of writings found in the early years of the Irish Literary Revival — but what is strange is that the document is dated 13 November 1921, a period long after the Literary Revival reached its peak. If the history of the Irish nationalist cause is taken into account, however, and more particularly the history of Arthur Griffith's career as a politician, the date is far more significant.

On 30 October 1921 Lloyd George and Arthur Griffith met at Winston Churchill's house to discuss the former's appearance on 17 November before the National Unionist Conference in Liverpool. Lloyd George wanted "personal assurances" from Griffith that in return for taking a strong stance on the issue of Irish unity he would receive the agreement of the Irish Delegates attending a conference called by the British government to the inclusion of their country in the British Empire and to allegiance toward the Crown. Griffith, who cared more for the unity of his country than what he viewed as ceremonial allegiance, agreed to give Lloyd George these assurances, speaking in his capacity as Chairman of the Irish Delegation.

Between that meeting and Griffith's commitment to paper of their understandings, there occurred a series of events which suggested that by 9 November Lloyd George had changed his mind, and was consenting to a proposal to allow six counties of Ireland under the jurisdiction of the Northern Commission to remain independent. When Sir James Craig, the Premier of Northern Ireland, and his cabinet refused to discuss an All-Ireland Parliament, but proposed instead two separate bodies, Northern and Southern Parliaments with equal powers, Lloyd George asked Griffith to aid him by agreeing to a compromise in which there would be one parliament, but Ulster would have the right to remove itself from that body within twelve months.

By this time Griffith was in a dilemma. He gave qualified assurances, but Lloyd George asked for more, based on their earlier conversations. On 13 November Griffith was shown a document which summarized his original conversation with Lloyd George, and on the basis of its contents, he agreed once again to settlement within the Empire and allegiance to the Crown, and he also consented to a request that he not openly oppose the proposal for Partition.

When a new "Irish Memorandum" was sent to the British on 22 November, it was drafted by Erskine Childers, George Gavan Duffy, and Robert Barton rather than by Griffith. It insisted upon the essential unity of Ireland even if that stand meant the failure of the Conference, the loss of an Irish Parliament, and the risk of war. The war came, a campaign of violence which turned into a bitter civil conflict. Before it had ended in April 1923, over 200 people were killed and about 1000 wounded. What this dark period in Ireland's history needed was a spark of national unity. And that was what Stephens sought to give his country in his next works of fiction. It was not to be an idealized portrait — his characters possessed all the ordinary human foibles — but it was a particularly Irish one, drawing upon the country's ancient legends.

Beginning with a belief that the ancient Gaelic tales represent an integral part of a national culture, Stephens offers, in the "Unity" typescript, an introduction to *Táin Bó Cuailnge*, the Ulster epic which, he contends, contains "all Ireland." According to most Irish scholars, *Táin Bó Cuailnge*, "The Cattle Raid at Cooley," was a tale told in the eighth century. Some of the verse passages in the story, however, may be at least two hundred years older than this. It underwent modification in the tenth century, and was first found in written form in two manuscripts, The Book of the Dun Cow (1100) and The Book of Leinster (1150); a later version, in incomplete form, is contained in The Yellow Book of Lecan (1391). The events of "The Cattle Raid" are pre-Christian, however. It is a record of heroes in horse-chariots whose virtues of truthfulness, loyalty, and fortitude are extolled. These pagan heroes die violently and gloriously for their clan, their king, or their pride. Christian elements have been inserted into some of the tales, probably by the monks who copied the stories; for example, in one tale, the death of a king is said to be the result of his anger over the news of Christ's crucifixion — his distress causes him to jump up quickly, dislodging a foreign body in his head received during battle.

Calling the *Táin* the "greatest epic in the world except perhaps the Mahabarata," Stephens raises his country's myths above those of the Greeks syllogistically: given that the Greek legends are philosophical questions about life, while the Irish legends are lyrical representations of life, and that it is easier to create philosophy than to create good art, then the Greeks' myths are not as difficult to create and, by extension, are not as great as the Gaelic epics. The premises may be shaky, but the conclusion is clear: Stephens is calling for a literary renaissance, a rebirth of the old tales so that they may form the basis for a distinctly Irish culture.

The manuscript closes with a challenge: "To Caesar what is his; to all men their own, and to us what is really ours, but if we will not accept and conserve and add to what is really ours then we must remain material and spiritual beggars in a world that has no use at all for poor relations."[2] Stephens had picked up his own gauntlet several years before writing this essay. In the period between 1918 and 1921, *Reincarnations* and *Irish Fairy Tales* were written and published, and two novels were begun which were to serve as a preface to his version of the *Táin, Deirdre* and *In the Land of Youth*. Actually, in order to serve the Irish Literary Revival, Stephens had been preparing himself since at least 1905. During this period he had studied Gaelic, consulted with Irish scholars, and read numerous articles on saga material. He knew the work of Kuno Meyer, Osborn Bergin, Douglas Hyde, and Standish Hayes O'Grady, and their translations provided him with the plot structures from which he elaborated his unique versions of the ancient Gaelic tales.³ Edmund Curtis first introduced him to the translation of the *Táin* made by Joseph Dunn, and Richard Best lent him his copy of *Silva Gadelica*, a collection of ancient tales given in Gaelic and English.

By the time he began his adaptations in fiction, Stephens could make use of four of the Irish saga cycles. The first, and perhaps best known, the *Táin* or, as it is also called, the Ulster or Red Branch cycle, relates the events leading up to the war between King Conachúr of Ulster and Queen Maeve of Connacht and includes the tales of Cúchulinn, the champion of the Red Branch. The others are the Fenian cycle, describing the life and deeds of Fionn Mac Cumhaill and his son Oisín, and centered around the kingdoms of Leinster and Munster; a mythological cycle, with stories relating to the *Tuatha dé Danaan* ("the People of the goddess Dana"), in which Ireland's history is traced from earliest times to the period of Christianity; and the various historical cycles, consisting of stories about Irish kings who are said to have reigned between the third century B.C. and the eighth century A.D.

IRISH FAIRY TALES (1920)

This is a collection of tales from three of the above cycles. "The Boyhood of Fionn," "The Birth of Bran," "Oisín's Mother," "The Little Brawl at Allen," "The Carl of the Drab Coat," and "The Enchanted Cave of Cesh Corran" are Fenian cycle stories; "The Story of Tuan Mac Cairill" is mythological; "The Wooing of Becfola," "Becuma of the White Skin," and "Mongan's Frenzy" are historical, although there are mythological components to the three stories.

In a letter dated 31 May 1913, Stephens wrote his friend, W. T. H. Howe, apparently in response to the latter's suggestion that he prepare a volume of Irish fairy tales: "It interests me a good deal. I would, of course, have to entirely write them and am sure I would enjoy doing so."⁴ In a second letter dated 30 December 1913, Stephens writes: "as to the Fairy & Hero books — If you are still of the same mind I will prepare & send you the first chapter of each of these. I begin to fancy that I would enjoy writing them."⁵ The book which evolved from these initial suggestions and responses, however, was not the one originally conceived by Howe. Stephens makes this point clear in a note written in Howe's copy of *Irish Fairy Tales* in which he thanks him for suggesting that he write fairy tales for children, but adds that "it is not a book for children at all, but, also, it would not have been a book at all, but that your letter switched my mind to your direction, & to the direction of these and such like tales."[6]

Between 1913 and 1918, Stephens was developing a conception of folk and fairy tales which would guide his rewriting of saga material in *Irish Fairy Tales*, *Deirdre*, and *In the Land of Youth*. His ideas are expressed in two undated typescripts, "On the Art of Writing" and "A Note on Fairyland," in which he develops a contrast between fairy and folk lore.[7] According to Stephens, the fairy tale deals with epistemological matters, basic questions of life and death, while the folk tale is concerned with "sensual wish fulfillments," that is, the "marginal evasions of the daily grind." Stephens associates the material of the fairy tale with that of dreams, and in contrast to this union he links folklore and daydreams. The latter material is found to be "properly unutilizable," but Stephens indicates that it is often employed by writers of stories in which weakness miraculously overpowers strength, for example, stories utilizing the plot of David and Goliath or Cinderella. These stories are folk tales by his definition, daydreams which should not be written in a realistic style for "if David be as strong in the head as Goliath is in the arm, the tale of a giants frustration can be moving & splendid — but two giants are concerned. If, as the story admits, Cinderella has beauty, she is already one up on her ugly sisters, & needs no fairy godmother to unash [sic] her — the first young man that passes will do very well. . . ." On the other hand, true fairy tales, as opposed to folk tales which have been transmitted and modified by the peasants who tell them, deal with death and life after death. They are "an attempt to tell where we go and what happens to us when we die."

It is thus with a serious aim in mind that he began the creation of his set of fairy tales for adults. It is not surprising, then, that Stephens has written, "I think the first 156 pages of this book are as good as my best work." These pages would include five short stories, "The Story of Tuan Mac Cairill,"

"The Boyhood of Fionn," "The Birth of Bran," "Oisín's Mother," and "The Wooing of Becfola."[8] All but the last are marked by a seriousness of tone and purpose in contrast to the five humorous stories which complete the volume.

In April 1919, Lady Gregory recorded her impression of the first short story:

> I went in the evening to hear Stephens read some of his new short stories. . . . Stephens read the opening of his Tain Stories, Tuan MacCarrell, who is to tell the tales. I thought it extraordinarily fine, the changing from tired and decrepit man to stag, to hawk, to salmon, with their joy in earth, water, air. And he has made even the coming of Parthalon and the passing of his people living and fine, remembered by the lonely man who had outlived them. He sat, as "A.E." says, "quite like a little gnome, wetting his finger at his mouth to turn each page, his face lighting up with the glory of his tale."[9]

Scél Tuáin maic Cairull do Finnén Maige Bile inso sís, "Tuan Mac Cairill's Story to Finnian of Moville," is an account of invasions of Ireland starting at the time of the Biblical Flood. In this account the first invasion consists of Partholon and his followers who come to Ireland from Greece after the Flood. After they are destroyed by a plague, they are replaced by Neimheadth, son of Pan, and his people who are in turn challenged by new invaders, the Fomorians from Africa. The Fir-Bolgs, a people who were once in bondage at Thrace and forced there to carry earth in bags, next invade the island and battle with the *Tuatha dé Danaan*, a cultivated people who emigrate to Ireland from the North. Finally, from Scythia, the Milesians come to seize control of Ireland.[10]

The legend is told as a frame story in which the abbot Finnian arrives in Moville and is told by his followers that a wealthy warrior there will not let them into his house but has "left them fasting there over Sunday." The abbot comforts his followers by predicting that a good man will come and tell them the ancient history of Ireland. The next morning a cleric comes who invites them to his hermitage. After prayers he introduces himself as Tuan, son of Cairill, son of Muredach, and Tuan, son of Starn, son of Sera. Finnian asks him to relate the events he has witnessed in Ireland. Tuan objects that he wishes to "meditate upon the Word of God," but Finnian convinces him that he should tell his adventures. Tuan's narration then includes the story of the invasions of Ireland.

In Stephens' short story, the powerful warrior and the meditative cleric are merged as a single character with the traits of the former and the genealogy of the latter. Stephens' Tuan is no longer a holy man; rather he is an opponent of the "new" religion, and thus his battle with the abbot represents the conflict between paganism and Christianity in ancient Ireland. In the short story, Tuan locks Finnian out, but when he and his servants become worried about the starving abbot, Finnian triumphs and Tuan succumbs to the psychological warfare to the extent of asking for religious instruction.

In the ancient version of Tuan's story, when Nemed and his people arrive, Tuan avoids meeting the settlers because he is "hairy, clawed, withered, grey, naked, wretched, miserable." Stephens adds his own section concerning the emotions felt by Tuan as he lives alone, becoming a beast in order to live with beasts — his joy when he sees Nemed's ships and his horror when he sees his reflection in a stream. The passage describing Tuan's reaction to his image illustrates how Stephens is able to take the seven adjectives from the legend and turn them into a picture as shocking to the narrator and his audience as it is to the reader:

> I saw that I was hairy and tufty and bristled as a savage boar; that I was lean as a stripped bush; that I was greyer than a badger; withered and wrinkled like an empty sack; naked as a fish; wretched as a starving crow in winter; and on my fingers and toes there were great curving claws, so that I looked like nothing that was known, like nothing that was animal or divine.[11]

According to *Scél Tuáin*, Tuan ages as a stag, passes into the shape of a wild boar consciously, then lives as a hawk, and finally as a salmon. He is happy in his metamorphosed shape and able to outwit fishermen's nets and spears until, he tells the abbot, God deems his capture by King Cairill's men and his subsequent rebirth as a human being. He also informs Finnian that he has been baptized by St. Patrick and that he believes in God. Finnian and Tuan then celebrate mass together. In Stephens' version, Tuan becomes a boar not by *willing* the change but after *dreaming* he is one. He also dreams himself into becoming a hawk and a fish. Stephens adds to his version of the story a long passage on the joys of being a salmon, eliminates mention of God's responsibility for Tuan's capture, and does not say that Tuan has been baptized by St. Patrick because he is portrayed as a pagan; thus Tuan can be baptized by Finnian, a ceremony symbolic of the triumph of the Christian religion over the ancient sects. Stephens also adds a final salute to Tuan, suggesting that he may yet live.

This gesture, like the affectionate farewell to Mary Makebelieve at the end of *The Charwoman's Daughter*, is indicative of the author's feelings toward his character and toward the story as a whole. In two letters to Howe dated February 1921, Stephens writes:

I am delighted with your appreciation of the Fairy Tales. But I implore you to read the first story twice. Read it aloud, if that can be done. It was meant to be so read. I swear it is a wonderful piece of work, & if nobody praises it but myself I'll burst with rage.

But when I advised you to read the first story, it is because I consider that one as especially excellent in a miraculously all-round excellence. . . . the "Story of Tuan mac Cairill" is a collossal and terrific, and unsurpassable, top-hole story, and I shall expect to hear from you in parallel terms; for I am at work, and if an artist is not praised he gets the jigs and then the blues and next the dumps, and after that he becomes a patriot and is hanged to the tune of the Old Cow Died Of.[12]

After finishing "The Story of Tuan," Stephens began work on the Fenian tales included in the collection. For "The Boyhood of Fionn," he consulted a variety of background materials in order to rework and combine two legends. *Macgnímartha Finn*, "Fionn's Boyhood Deeds," was written down in the twelfth century from oral folk tales. Written about the same period was *Agallamh na Senórach in so*, "The Colloquy with the

Ancients," in which Caoilte recounts his leader's exploits and tells St. Patrick of Fionn's fight with his arch enemy, Aodh.[13]

Stephens' short story begins with Fionn as a child being raised apart from his widowed mother in the seclusion of a forest. Here he receives information concerning the events and politics of the Irish high court from his nurse-guardians and an education which consists of learning how to run like the animals of the forest and how to swim with the fish of the marshes. These feats will protect him from his father's enemies, the clan Morna. Fionn is eventually sent away with a band of poets, and with this group he receives a more cultural education. But after his sojourn with the poets, there is more survival training in the jungle-world of nature from his uncle, a robber, and from his guardians. Following this apprenticeship, Fionn faces a number of increasingly more difficult tests. He meets and bests a group of jealous older boys; he challenges and triumphs over his mother's second husband, the King of Kerry, in seven games of chess; and at Tara he offers to defend Art, the High King, against the grandson of the Lord of the Underworld, Aillen Mac Midna. On his way to meet Aillen, he is offered a magic spear by his robber-uncle; the stench of this sword helps to keep him from being soothed to sleep by Aillen's music. He succeeds, as Nera will succeed in Stephens' novel, *In the Land of Youth*; indeed, the two stories spring from a common base in folklore — an ambitious young man accepts a challenge on All Hallows' Eve to walk into the darkness of the night and face the evil spirits.

Fionn slays Aillen and returns to Tara to claim his price, command of the Fianna of Ireland. His old enemy, Goll Mac Morna, faced with the choice of accepting Fionn as his leader or leaving the country, agrees to forsake his enmity and join with Fionn. Thus far Fionn's tests have involved combat. His final challenge comes, however, from a poet. He must cook but not eat the Salmon of Knowledge caught by his master, thereby demonstrating his strength of will over the "strong desire" of youth. This event takes place while Fionn lives with Finegas, a wise old poet who resides on a river bank because "a poem is a revelation, and it is by the brink of running water that poetry is revealed to the mind." Finegas adds to Fionn's education by teaching him the art of poetry:

. . . he thought over all the poet taught him, and his mind

dwelt on the rules of metre, the cunningness of words, and the need for a clean, brave mind. But in his thousand thoughts he yet remembered the Salmon of Knowledge as eagerly as his master did. He already venerated Finegas because of his great learning, his poetic skill, for a hundred reasons; but, looking on him as the ordained eater of the Salmon of Knowledge, he venerated him to the edge of measure. Indeed he loved as well as venerated this master because of his unfailing kindness, his readiness to teach, and his skill in teaching.[14]

Certainly, cadence and language have traditionally been the province of poets, but the need for spiritual qualities is not merely a historical note; it is revelatory of Stephens' views on poetry. Ultimately, it is the wise and kindly Finegas who tells Fionn that the prophecy states that it is Fionn who will eat the Salmon of Knowledge.

The next short story has its origin in a legend contained in The Yellow Book of Lecan. The story of Bran's birth explains the highly unusual familial relationship between Fionn and his dogs, Bran and Sceólan. According to this tale, the dogs are his cousins, conceived by his aunt Tuiren when she is under an enchantment placed upon her by her husband's other-world sweetheart. The translation of the story provided by Lady Gregory in *Gods and Fighting Men* is faithful to the legend, even to its solemn narration of an odd and potentially hilarious situation.[15] In Stephens' hands, the focus of the story and the tone entirely change.

"The Birth of Bran" becomes a delightful short story of a man, Fergus Fionnlaith, who hates dogs. After Fionn's aunt Tuiren is turned into a hound by Uct Dealv, her husband's ex-sweetheart, she is given to Fergus by Uct Dealv who assumes that Fergus will mistreat the animal. Because of his fear of Fionn, however, the man who dislikes dogs becomes the man who is good to them. When the dog shivers, Fergus learns from a servant that dogs must be hugged and kissed. He does this with some hesitation at first, but learns readily enough to love the dog. By the time the spell is broken, the hound has already given birth to the two puppies, Bran and Sceólan. These are sent to Fionn, "and he loved them for ever after, for they were loyal and affectionate, as only dogs can be, and they were as intelligent as human beings." Tuiren weds the warrior-poet who loved her all the time, Uct Dealv regains her lost sweetheart, and Fergus, who has taken to his bed upon the loss of his beloved dog, is given a pup by Fionn. All the "couples" live happily ever after.

Throughout this and other short stories in *Irish Fairy Tales*, Stephens provides a humorous note by utilizing the ancient Gaelic endearments. When Uct Dealv is talking of her lover Iollan to her sister, she says: "He said I was the Berry of the Mountain, the Star of Knowledge, and the Blossom of the Raspberry." Her sister protests that men "always say the same thing," and perhaps they do, for Fergus talking about his hound to the servants sounds much like Iollan; he tells them that the hound is "the Queen of Creatures, the Pulse of his Heart, and the Apple of his Eye."

The tale of Oisín's mother is told both in The Book of Leinster and another ancient Gaelic manuscript described as Egerton 161. The material in the Leinster manuscript contains only two quatrains dealing with the birth of Oisín; however, the Egerton manuscript holds a forty-nine quatrain poem, *Ag so sios seanchas agus oileamhain Oisin Mhic Fhinn*, "Here follows legendary lore and the manner of Oisín's bringing up."[16] If his sources are compared with his short story, it is clear that Stephens has created a new, poignant tale of love gained and lost rather than presenting a faithful literary translation.

This is also true of "The Wooing of Becfola": Stephens' tale is not a faithful reproduction of the legend, *Tochmarc Becfola*, but a newly-fashioned parody of fairy tale romances. Stephens' source for the legend is Standish Hayes O'Grady's translation, but while his short story follows the action set forth in the translation, this rather grim tale of adultery and intrigue becomes a lighthearted comedy based on the absurdity of those characters in fairy tales who blithely marry strangers about whom they know nothing.[17] Becfola's husband, King Dermod, is portrayed as a dignified, taciturn man in the legend; Stephens makes him a quite ordinary creature with a plodding sense of humor and a fatal obliviousness to the machinations of a strong-willed woman.

"The Wooing of Becfola," "The Little Brawl at Allen," "The Carl of the Drab Coat," and "The Enchanted Cave of Cesh Corran" are stories with a comic battle, magical intervention, and happy ending.[18]

In Stephens' hands, "The Little Brawl at Allen" becomes an exuberant story of how a banquet given by Fionn turns into a battle in which all the guests fight until the court poets, the only possible umpires, are able to effect a truce. In the legend entitled "The Carl of the Drab Coat," Fionn is challenged by Cael, son of the King of Thessaly, to produce his swiftest runner. Fionn sets out to find one of his warriors, but on the way meets a very unprepossessing giant, Carl of the Drab Coat. Carl offers to run the race and persuades Fionn that only he can win. Cael, at first indignant over the insult implied in a match with a dumpy giant, finally agrees to a sixty-mile contest. In the course of the hilarious race, Carl builds a hut, catches a boar, gives Cael an hour's head start, catches up with Cael then drops behind to eat blackberries, sews on his torn coat-tails, and then settles down to winning.

Once again Stephens employs Gaelic endearments to comic effect. Here the unlikely object of affection is the giant's rival, whom he calls "my pulse" and "my darling," much as Fergus Fionnliath has ennobled his hound. That Carl is an unheroic hero is brought home in Stephens' description of his behavior after the race. Unlike the courtly rewards given to most Gaelic warriors, Carl's request is for "a store of blackberries squashed, crushed, mangled, democratic, ill-looking":

> Into the centre of the mess of blackberries he discharged a barrel of meal, and he mixed the two up and through, and round and down, until the pile of white-black, red-brown, slibber-slobber reached up to his shoulders. Then he commenced to paw and impel and project and cram the mixture into his mouth, and between each mouthful he sighed a contented sigh, and during every mouthful he gurgled an oozy gurgle.[19]

When his rival swoops down on Carl in this unappetizing position, he finds his head smashed off and then thrown back in joint, a yearly rent extracted from him, and a rude return to his awaiting ship. Only after these feats does the grotesque Carl reveal himself in his true shape as "one of splendour and delight," the ruler of the *Shí* (fairy fort) of Rath Cruachan.

"The Enchanted Cave of Cesh Corran" is a *bruidhean tale*,

a story, that is, which relates how a hero is enticed into a magical dwelling and how he is maltreated there. Stephens begins his short story with a descriptive statement concerning Fionn and his companion-enemy Goll Mac Morna. When Fionn's insatiable curiosity gets the Fianna in trouble it is Goll who loyally rescues them. This time, trouble takes the form of the daughters of the King of the Shí of Cesh Corran who plot to trap Fionn. Stephens has great fun with his portrayal of the women who are ugly beyond belief:

> Their hair was black as ink and tough as wire: it stuck up and poked out and hung down about their heads in bushes and spikes and tangles. Their eyes were bleary and red. Their mouths were black and twisted, and in each of these mouths there was a hedge of curved yellow fangs. They had long scraggy necks that could turn all the way round like the neck of a hen. . . . Their bodies were covered with a bristle of hair and fur and fluff, so that they looked like dogs in some parts and like cats in others, and in other parts again they looked like chickens. They had moustaches poking under their noses and woolly wads growing out of their ears, so that when you looked at them the first time you never wanted to look at them again, and if you had to look at them a second time you were likely to die of the sight.[20]

Stephens' examples of historical stories include the two with which he ends his volume. In 1175, the Norman Invasion of Ireland ended the reign of the Irish high kings, and began the rule of lords. Between 1200 and 1600, there was renewed interest in the old tales of Fionn, Deirdre, and Cúchulinn, but added to these favorites were new adventure and romantic tales such as *Eachtra Airt Mheic Cuinn*, "The Adventures of Art son of Conn," and *Compert Mongáin ocus Serc Duibe-Lacha do Mongán*, "The Conception of Mongán and Dub-Lach's Love for Mongán."[21] These two stories are represented in *Irish Fairy Tales* under the titles of "Becuma of the White Skin" and "Mongan's Frenzy."

Becuma is a woman of "The Many-Coloured Land" who has run away from her husband to live with another man.

Banished to earth for this deed, she succeeds by trickery and lies to enthrall Conn, the High King of Ireland. When Conn first sees Becuma he asks her a number of questions, "for it is not every day that a lady drives from the sea, and she wearing a golden fringed cloak of green silk through which a red satin smock peeped at the openings." This reference to a king asking questions of a strange woman is not unlike the story of Becfola and King Dermod. Conn, despite a policy in opposition to Dermod, fares equally poorly even when he asks questions because his lady does not tell the truth. Becuma secures the King's marriage proposal and his promise to banish his son from Tara for a year, but after many adventures, Art succeeds in bringing about the banishment of Becuma and thus saves Ireland from a famine.

"Mongan's Frenzy" is told within the framework of two storytellers. Cairidè tells the tale of Mongan to the Abbot of the Monastery of Moville, but within the tale Mongan himself tells a story of his earlier days to his wife Brótiarna. By the inclusion of the Abbot of Moville as a character in "Mongan's Frenzy," Stephens links his last story with his first, "The Story of Tuan Mac Cairill," in which the Abbot also appears.

"Mongan's Frenzy," when compared with the legend as translated by Kuno Meyer in *The Voyage of Bran*, serves as a good demonstration of Stephens' ability to recast a traditional story. He has added the Abbot of Moville to the story in order to link his first and last short stories; he has provided a psychological analysis of the relationship between Mongan and Brótiarna, concluding that Brótiarna's troubles are those of people "who love the great ones of life and strive to equal themselves where equality is not possible"; he has enlarged and made more grotesque the legend's description of the Hag of the Mill and of Mananán's dog; he has added the comic conversations among the main characters, the songs composed on the way to and from King Branduv's household, and the funny ending of the story; and he has provided a scene at the feast of Moy Lifé which has the movement and color of a Brueghel painting.

It is appropriate that the stories of Tuan and Mongan should serve as the frame for a collection of Irish tales, for if Tuan's tale involves shape-changing, Mongan's deals with transmigration. Mongan and Fionn are not dissimilar figures. Like King Arthur, Mongan and Fionn are chieftains who, despite impres-

sive magical powers, lose their wives; Mongan is the only one
of the three to recover his spouse. Mongan is frequently called
the reborn Fionn in the ancient Gaelic legends; in "Mongan's
Frenzy," Stephens has indicated knowledge of this in his ending.
Another interrelationship among the heroes of the Irish sagas
is the association of Fionn, Mongan, and Cúchulinn with Lugh,
the Celtic god of light. Cúchulinn and Fionn are sons of a
god and a mortal; both answer to their adult names after
they have killed, in one case, a hound, in the other, a group
of hostile boys. Cúchulinn is associated with Lugh in many
tales, and in one of three versions of the hero's birth in the
ancient manuscript, The Book of the Dun Cow, he is said to
be Lugh reborn as a mortal. Like Lugh, Fionn has an opponent
who is a fiery, one-eyed warrior. Mongan, "the reborn Fionn,"
is also said to be the son of a mortal and the god of the
sea, Mananán, who is a "shape-shifter," that is, one who is
able to change shape. Thus, a linkage might be traced from
Lugh to his rebirths as Fionn, Cúchulinn, and, through Fionn
and Mananán, to Mongan.

Although *Irish Fairy Tales* is a departure in setting and characterization from the earlier fiction of Stephens, there are certain
thematic similarities to be found. Once again fantasy (magical
dwellings, shape-changing, disguised gods) is combined with
reality (conflicting emotions of lovers, boasting conversations
between rivals, devotion to children). It is appropriate that
the stories of Fionn dominate the collection because he embraced
both worlds. Fionn was a hero, a giant, a descendant of the
gods; but he was also, like Stephens, a father, a husband,
and a man who loved "the music of what happens."

DEIRDRE (1923)

The Deirdre legend is found in two Gaelic versions. An older
tale *Longes Mac n'Uislenn*, "The Exile of the Sons of Uisneac,"
is recorded in The Book of the Dun Cow and The Book of
Leinster, twelfth-century manuscripts, and The Yellow Book
of Lecan, dated around 1391. These manuscripts contain rendi-
tions of a tale which was told orally at least as early as the
ninth century. A medieval tale, *Oidheadh Chloinne h'Uisneach*,
"The Violent Death of the Children of Uisneac," is found

in the Glenmasan and other Advocate Library manuscripts, dating probably from the late fifteenth century.

In both versions Cathbad, the king's druid, foretells that a new-born child will bring destruction to Ulster. Against the advice of his nobles, Conachúr, King of Ulster, allows the child, Deirdre, to live, and he announces his intention to marry her. At the time of the marriage, Deirdre elopes with a young warrior, Naoise, son of Uisneac, and his two brothers. The four flee to Scotland, but they are tricked into returning to Ireland by a vengeful Conachúr. Fergus Mac Roy, stepfather of Conachúr and one of the great Ultonian warriors, guarantees their safety, but he is compelled to attend a banquet while his sons and the exiles march to Emain Macha, the capital of Ulster. Here, the sons of Uisneac are brutally murdered by Conachúr's henchman. At this point the two versions differ markedly. In the older manuscripts, Conachúr seizes Deirdre, who is forced to live with him for one year. Enraged by her mourning, he sends her to live for a year with her husband's murderer. On the way, seated between Conachúr and the murderer, Deirdre kills herself by jumping out of the chariot and smashing her head on a stone. In the medieval version, Deirdre commits suicide immediately after the murder of the three sons of Uisneac by drinking the dead Naoise's blood.

Stephens had a good working knowledge of the various Deirdre legends. He also had read two well-known books, Patrick Dinneen's translation of Geoffrey Keating's *History of Ireland*, in which the older version of the legend as it is recorded in The Book of Leinster is told, and Douglas Hyde's *A Literary History of Ireland*, which provides both the older and the medieval versions.[22] Furthermore, the story was popular during the period of the Irish Literary Revival, and Stephens' contemporaries had utilized the legend in various literary modes. Many composed poems, several offered fictional accounts, and three writers with whom Stephens was friendly, AE, William Butler Yeats, and John Synge, wrote plays on the topic, all of which were produced prior to Stephens' novel.

Unlike his literary associates, however, Stephens fills in material from other tales where he feels that it is needed artistically. Like the saga version found in The Book of Leinster, Stephens' story begins at the house of Felimid Mac Dall, poet and story maker to the King of Ulster, Conachúr Mac Nessa. However, unlike the manuscript, Stephens begins with a humorous, and apparently historically possible, anecdote. When Conachúr arrives to spend the night at Felimid's house, he asks for his bed-rights with the poet's wife, and he is refused on the grounds that she is giving birth to a child. True to the legend, Stephens' king is warned to beware of the new-born baby, Deirdre, but it is Bricriu, a quarrelsome noble, who objects to the child. Thus Conachúr, who obviously dislikes Bricriu and finds him cowardly, has all the more justification for ignoring the dreaded prophecy.

In the ancient saga, two questions are posed, and the answers each constitute a part of the tale. The first question is: what caused the exile of the sons of Uisneac? In *Deirdre*, Stephens deals with the answer to this question in Part One of the novel in which the girl's upbringing and her meeting with Naoise and his brothers are narrated. In the Leinster tale, the King takes Deirdre as a baby out of Emain Macha, to be raised in seclusion by him and a nurse, a woman gifted for "satire." The saga says, "she talked with Deirdre, and explained, and they smiled in irony." In Stephens' version, Lavarcham is the conversation-woman to the King, and it is she alone who raises the girl, teaching her the arts and womanly virtues and telling her stories about the court. Deirdre does not see Conachúr as a child; it is Lavarcham who reports the girl's progress to the King.

Stephens elects to add to his story a detail not present in versions of the Deirdre story, that Maeve, Conachúr's queen, left Ulster during Deirdre's adolescence. Stephens pictures the queen as she is in many of the tales of the Ulster saga. A spirited, warlike woman, she demands three qualities in a husband, and being typically argumentative she couches her requirements negatively: the man must not be cowardly, must not be niggardly, and must not be jealous. Although Conachúr fulfills the first two conditions, he fails the third, for which Maeve leaves him bag, baggage, and army. The inclusion of this incident in *Deirdre* is a bold stroke, an opportunity to sketch one of the leading figures of the *Táin Bó Cuailnge*.

In the ancient legend, the King kills a calf, and Deirdre, while watching a raven drink the blood of the calf in the snow, tells her nurse that she desires a man with "raven-black hair, the colour of blood on his cheeks and a snowwhite body."

Stephens rejects the starkness of this incident. His Deirdre, lonely in her imprisonment, slips into the woods and wanders onto the camp site of the three sons of Uisneac. Although Stephens says that girls are to blame for love affairs, he makes this remark in a good-natured tone, quite unlike the ancient account of Deirdre's hysterical confrontation with Naoise in which she grabs him by the ears and shouts that she desires a "young bull" — a rather unique method of taking the bull by the horns. Stephens' hero is worried about his beloved's relationship to Conachúr, but it is as the King's ward, not the King's betrothed that she is viewed. Deirdre must come on her own initiative to meet him in the forest a second time at night, but it is Naoise who takes her arm and leads her away from the camp site.

Only after this night does Conachúr come to see his ward and, overwhelmed by her beauty, he announces he will marry her. Thus the marriage is not settled at birth as it is in the Gaelic legend and thus Deirdre pledges her love before the King proposes; Stephens, thereby, softens the aspect of treason present in the original tale. However, the girl must still confront Naoise with the news that the King wishes to marry her, and it is she who suggests that they run away over his objections.

The second question posed in the ancient legend asks: what caused the death of the sons of Uisneac? In Stephens' novel, Part Two begins with the King's plot to bring Deirdre and the sons of Uisneac back from Scotland and ends with the death of the four. Stephens opens this section with Conachúr and Lavarcham in conversation prior to a banquet for the nobles of Ulster. This occasion allows the King an opportunity to ask Lavarcham the news about Deirdre and the others, and thus the author is able to summarize the background material needed before the story can proceed. Stephens also takes the opportunity during the banquet scene to introduce the lovers, Emer and Cúchulinn. She is the proud, beautiful, and strong woman of the old tales; he, the easygoing and good-natured hero. The enmity between Ulster and Connacht is mentioned, and Fergus, who will later fight with Connacht against Conachúr, defends the Connachtmen. The novel proceeds, then, following the legend fairly closely up to the moment of the return of the exiles to Emain Macha.

In the legend it is reported without detail that the sons

of Uisneac and Fergus' sons, who served as sureties for their safety, are killed on the plains of Emain upon their arrival. Stephens, however, inserts a long, curiously comic, fight scene.

Stephens' extended description of the battle does not have its beginnings in the ancient legends, nor is it a part of the versions of the Deirdre story produced by his friends, AE, Yeats, Synge, and Lady Gregory. The fighting takes place off-stage in the first three; the retelling of the legend found in *Cuchulain of Muirthemne* includes only a sketch of the combat. A closer source is Stephens' account of the Easter Rising, *The Insurrection in Dublin*. Bravery, courage, lightheartedness — the essential qualities in battle of Naoise, Ardan, and Ainnle — are the attributes Stephens cites for the rebels of 1916. Those who fought in the Uprising faced impossible odds, displayed a selfless concern for others, and refused to surrender to their enemies. Stephens told one of the stories about the Volunteers in his account of the Uprising: an Irish garrison refused to surrender to the English officer in command because "they were not there to surrender. They were there to be killed. The garrison consisted of fifty men, and the story said that fifty were killed."[23]

The sons of Uisneac battle cunningly, and it is only through the magic spell of Cathfa, the druid, that they are caught. The four exiles are imprisoned overnight, and the next morning, the King comes with their murderer. Stephens' execution scene in prison is a poignant moment:

"I shall be the first," said Ardan briskly. "I am first in every great deed," he explained to Conachúr.

"Hark to him!" Ainnle laughed. "Respect your elders, young person, and the heads of your family."

But Ardan appealed to Mainè.

"Let me be first, sweet sir," he pleaded. He turned confidingly to Conachúr. "I cannot bear to see my brothers killed," he said.[24]

Deirdre then sings her keen over the three bodies, but only the first line of a poem which is quite long in various versions of the saga is given, apparently because Stephens does not wish to mitigate the starkness of the scene. Although he rejects the older version of Deirdre's death, Stephens is courageous enough to utilize the medieval version to end his tale. In AE's play, Deirdre collapses, presumably of heart failure; in Yeats' and Synge's versions, she kills herself with a knife. Stephens' Deirdre sips the blood of her dead lover and dies.

Stephens deals with the Deirdre story not just as an isolated legend, but as one of the *remscela*, the many related tales which are background for the *Táin Bó Cuailnge*. His awareness of these other tales allows him to make appropriate references to them within the context of the novel. For example, his introduction of Conachúr includes some material both factual and comic on his mother, Assa-Nessa, her marriage to Cathfa, and her subsequent marriage to Fergus. It is apparent that Stephens knows the tale in The Book of Leinster entitled *Scéla Conchoboir maic Nessa*, "The Tidings of Conachúr Mac Nessa." This story includes material on Nessa's two marriages, a confirmation of Conachúr's *ius primae noctis* and other bed-rights, a description of the three royal houses at Emain Macha, and specific references to Conall Cearnach and Bricriu. Stephens is also aware that in the saga manuscripts Conachúr is referred to as the son of Fachtna as well as the son of Cathfa. He diplomatically leaves the matter unsettled by saying a son was born to Cathfa and Nessa, but that "there are some who say, however, that Fachtna the Mighty had been the leman of Nessa, and that it was he who was the father of Conachúr instead of Cathfa."

Another *remscela*, *Cath Boinde*, "The Battle of the Boyne," furnishes Stephens with material on Eochaid Feidleach's daughters, four of whom married Conachúr, and the information that Maeve, the final daughter to marry the King, left him "through the pride of mind" and returned to her father who gave her the kingdom of Connacht to rule with her consort Ailill. *Fled Bricrenn*, "The Feast of Bricriu," introduces material on the venomous-tongued Bricriu, the troublemaker of the court, and on the women of the court mentioned by Lavarcham in *Deirdre*. In this tale, three women, Fedelm of the Fresh Heart, Lendubair, and Emer, have a "war of words" over who is the most noble and beautiful and who really has the most heroic husband. The imperious Emer wins, just as she cows the court in Stephens' banquet scene.

Even material about Emer's husband Cúchulinn, from stories which form a legend in themselves, is brought naturally and easily into *Deirdre*. When the three sons of Uisneac talk around the fire, they mention fragments of stories concerning their hero, stories which are told fully in *Macgnímrada Con Culainn*, "The Boyhood Deeds of Cúchulinn," and *Tochmarc Emire*, "The Wooing of Emer." In the fireside discussion, later battles are hinted at between Cúchulinn and Fergus, and Cúchulinn and Ferdiad, accounts of which appear in the main body of the *Táin Bó Cuailnge*. In Part Two of the novel, Stephens says that Cúchulinn and Conall Cearnach surrendered their powers as equal kings to Conachúr, "who was now known and described as Emperor of Ulster." This story is told in *Mesca Ulad*, "The Intoxication of the Ultonians," in which Conachúr's aides talk Cúchulinn and Fintan into yielding their portions of rule for one year to him, thus making Conachúr "arch-king" of Ulster.

In a note dated 2 February 1924, Stephens writes to W. T. H. Howe asking him to add these lines to his copy of *Deirdre*:

> After great heat great cold comes following!
> Tiresias was lost by the daughter of Maelscháclin,
>   the king;
> By Gránia of high Ben Bulban in the North was
>   Diarmuid lost;
> The strong sons of Uisneach, who never submitted,
>   they fell by Deirdre.[25]

The note indicates that "these verses should properly end 'Deirdre'." In a letter dated three days later he adds that he regrets having forgotten his plan to use the poem as the ending of the book because it "would have so excellently finished that tale."[26] The lines are a slightly revised version of stanzas two through five of "The Red Man's Wife" which appeared in 1918 in *Reincarnations*.

The poem's reference to the Grainne-Diarmuid story is another indication of Stephens' grasp of interrelated mythic material, for the story has many connections with the Deirdre legend. Grainne, daughter of Cormac, is sought by Fionn, the warrior-leader of a large band. She loves Diarmuid, a young soldier of his troop, however, and she commands Diarmuid to carry her away. Diarmuid, unwilling to betray his leader, asks the advice of Oisín, Oscar, and Caoilte, who tell him to obey her order. The two lovers escape for a period of time, then return to Fionn's territory. While hunting unarmed one day with Fionn, Diarmuid is gored by a boar. Fionn can save him by carrying water to him in his cupped hands, but three times he spills the water, and Diarmuid dies.

In both the Deirdre and Grainne legends, the heroine rejects an older man, a leader of his people, for a young warrior-follower. The young man hesitates to betray his ruler, is shamed into agreeing to elope, and flees with the woman through a forest to a hiding place. The older man brings the lovers back by professing forgiveness, but brings about the death of the young man through treachery. James Carney has suggested that the Deirdre legend is the earliest Irish derivative of the British Tristan-Iseult legend, and he further compares these two stories with that of the Grainne tale.[27]

To compare *Deirdre* with its original source is an excellent method for observing how Stephens adapts his materials. He employs two different options: compression and expansion. As an example of the first, the following passage from the novel contains in abbreviated form material from several tales:

> They [Deirdre and the sons of Uisneac] may have met Cúchulinn there [Scotland], for it would be about that time that he was under the tuition of the female warrior and witch, Scatach; and, if so, they should have met his comrade Ferdiad also, he who was to assail the ford afterwards with what a hand! and it may have been during their exile that Cúchulinn fell in love with Scatach's daughter, and that the child was born who would receive such a woeful stroke on Báile's Strand.[28]

Douglas Hyde mentions an eighteenth-century version of *Foglaim con Culain* in which Cúchulinn finds the three sons of Uisneac and Deirdre at the house of Scatach.[29] They are homesick for news of Ireland and greet him warmly, showing him the Bridge of the Cliffs which they have learned to navigate. Cúchulinn's period with Scatach is recorded in several versions of *Tochmarc Emire*; he falls in love with the witch's daughter, Uactach, but the child mentioned by Stephens is Conla, a son of Scatach's enemy, Aoife, whom Cúchulinn overpowers. Conla is tragically killed by his father who does not recognize him in battle years later. The story of Ferdiad at the Ford comes from the Combat of Cúchulinn and Ferdiad told in the *Táin Bó Cuailnge*. Thus, in a few brief lines, Stephens refers to a larger body of Irish saga material when it serves no purpose to be more expansive.

On the other hand, he may tell a small portion of a tale in more detail than it was told originally. In the older versions of *Tochmarc Emire*, Bricriu suggests that when Conachúr claimed his traditional wedding night privilege with Emer, Cúchulinn was so angry that Conachúr was forced to waive his rights. To maintain his kingly pride, he spent the night in Emer's bed, but he was joined by Fergus who remained to safeguard Cúchulinn's honor. This story, which occupies only a few lines in a Gaelic manuscript becomes a portion of a long conversation between Conachúr and Lavarcham in Part Two of *Deirdre*. At first angry as he recalls that neither Fergus nor Cúchulinn was willing to accept his word that Emer would be safe, the King breaks into laughter as he tells Lavarcham of the discomforts of the night: a small bed occupied by three large, clothed adults and a sleeping Emer who kicked the King in the back with her knees and prodded him with her sharp elbows. Here, Stephens expands rather than shortens his background material, to obtain humorous results.

In a letter to W. T. H. Howe dated 8 June 1923, Stephens writes "About 'Deirdre.' I think it is the best thing I have done — It is the first book (complete in itself) of a story in 5 volumes to be called the 'Tain Bo', and although it is as old as time, it will be as modern as tomorrow's newspaper."[30] Indeed, Stephens saw in Deirdre many of the traits of the modern heroine. In his version of the ancient tale, Deirdre joins the line of lonely young women who rebel against their parents. She is the most rebellious of the four, running away from her guardian and refusing to marry a king. Like Caitilin Ni Murrachu, she is a beautiful woman raised in the sunshine and peace of the Irish countryside. Like Mary Makebelieve who talks to ducklings, Deirdre converses with birds in their nests. When she puts her arms around "the shaggy mare and her dear, shy foaleen," one remembers Mary Mac Cann hugging her donkey. Deirdre's maternal instinct is aroused when she meets Naoise, for she knows that she can be both mother and wife to him.

Deirdre's guardian, Lavarcham, has a face of "ivory and jet," an abbreviated description recalling Mrs. Makebelieve and the Thin Woman. All three women hold strong opinions on domestic matters and are able counselors on the subject of the warfare between men and women. The male characters in the first four novels are also related. The lodger, the demi-god Art, and Naoise are boyish, handsome, and heroic. The villainous Policeman and Conachúr are spiders, waiting to catch Mary and Deirdre in their webs.

His insertions of "modernity" in *Deirdre* and *Irish Fairy Tales* — the humanizing of the saga figures by explanations of their emotions, the addition of color and humor to the darker tales of treachery and murder, and the creation of dialogue which is comprehensible to the modern reader — do not prevent Stephens from maintaining the integrity of the legends by adhering to their essential plot and outlines. As Dorothy Hoare points out, "there is no sense of jar or transition."[31]

IN THE LAND OF YOUTH (1924)

Deirdre ends with the words, "So Far, the Fate of the Sons of Uisneac, and the Opening of the Great Táin." The second novel in Stephens' Táin, *In the Land of Youth*, consists of four interrelated tales, The Adventures of Nera, The Vision of Angus Óg, The Tale of Two Swineherds, and The Wooing of Etain, told in the court of Queen Maeve of Connacht.

The first part contains the story of Nera's adventures when he accepts the challenge of Naeve's consort, Ailill, to go out into the darkness on *Samhain* (All Hallow's Eve). It describes Nera's courageous deed of tying a withy on the foot of a corpse, his comradely act of securing water for the thirsty body which is not quite dead, his short stay with a woman of the *Shí* (fairy fort), and his return to warn his monarch of a plot against her court. When Nera returns to the court, his story prompts Maeve to explain the anger of the fairies by telling the tale of The Vision of Angus, son of the Dagda Mór and Boann. Interpolated in this story is a tale told by a character in it, Bove the magician, about the rivalry between the two swineherds, Friuc of Munster and Rucht of Connacht. Thus, the stories in Part One, which involve the Kingdoms of Connacht, Ulster, Munster, and Leinster, are told in a "Chinese-box" fashion: Nera's story provides the outside frame; within

it is Queen Maeve's story of The Vision of Angus; and within
that tale is Bove's story of The Two Swineherds. At the end
of Part One of the novel, Nera returns to the *Shí*; in Part
Two, Maeve, encouraged by the hearty reception of her audience
to her tale of Angus, tells the story of The Wooing of Etain.

Echtra Nerai, "The Adventures of Nera," appears in the Egerton 1782 manuscript and, with variants, in The Yellow Book
of Lecan.[32] It is interesting to note one example of how Stephens
has changed the tale without altering the basic outline of the
plot. The manuscript version, as translated by Kuno Meyer,
begins:

> One Halloween Ailill and Medb were in Rath Cruachan
> with their whole household. They set about cooking food.
> Two captives had been hanged by them the day before
> that. Then Ailill said: "He who would now put a withe
> round the foot of either of the two captives that are on
> the gallows, shall have a prize for it from me, as he may
> choose."[33]

Stephens has expanded this brief beginning into a description
of the Connacht court, an explanation of the meaning of *Samhain*,
and an inviting description of Maeve's feast. He also has created
the dialogue which precedes Ailill's challenge.

Stephens' Nera is more sympathetic than the character in
the legend on which he is modeled. In the saga there is no
description of Nera's feelings as he sets out to put the withy
around the foot of a dead man, there is no report of his reaction
when he returns to Cruachan and sees the burning tent and
beheaded bodies of his monarchs and friends, and there is
no mention of affection felt by him for the woman of the
Shí who takes him into her house.

Stephens also condenses material from the saga to suit his
needs. When Nera and the hanged captive go in search of
water, the Meyer translation of the tale reads:

> So they went to that house. Then they saw something. A
> lake of fire round that house. "There is no drink for us
> in this house", said the captive. "There is no fire without
> sparing in it ever. "Let us therefore go to the other house,
> which is nearest to us", said the captive. They went to

it then and saw a lake of water around it. "Do not go to that house!" said the captive. There is never a washing- nor a bathing-tub, nor a slop-pail in it at night after sleeping. "Let us still go to the other house", said the captive. "Now there is my drink in this house", said the captive. He let him down on the floor. He went into the house. There were tubs for washing and bathing in it, and a drink in either of them. Also a slop-pail on the floor of the house. He then drinks a draught of either of them and scatters the last sip from his lips at the faces of the people that were in the house, so that they all died. Henceforth, it is not good (to have) either a tub for washing or bathing, or a fire without sparing, or a slop-pail in a house after sleeping.[34]

This episode, which contains many primitive folkloric elements, is reduced by Stephens to a scene in which the author allows the pair to enter only one house and to which he adds the humor of having the occupants of the house in a state of shock at the sight of Nera carrying a corpse.

References in the saga story to a team of a lame man and a blind man who guard the treasure are retained and described by Stephens in a faithful fashion, but a humorous dialogue in which the men quarrel is added. Stephens keeps the use of the fruits of summer as proof of Nera's stay in the *Shí*, but he omits the woman's promise to Nera that she will bear a son in his absence. He ends his version of Nera's adventures with Nera's return to the *Shí*, although the original tale continues with two incidents involving cattle raids.

Maeve, as characterized by Stephens, is the imperious, proud woman pictured in the Ulster sagas. She is very aware of her beauty; as she says to Nera ". . . [I] am honey-haired, and there are some who think that I am sweet-cheeked and desirable." Her tale of the vision of Angus is important for it not only explains why that god from the kingdom of Ulster fights on Maeve's side in the Cattle Raid of Cooley, but it also demonstrates her own impetuous and warlike nature which triggers the war between Connacht and Ulster. Fergus is shown as a member of Maeve's court, although in the original saga material he appears in Cruachan only after Nera has left the *Shí*. The behavior of Maeve and Fergus suggests that they are already lovers, indicating that Stephens is acquainted with a legend, *Aided Fergusa Maicc roig*, "The Death of Fergus Mac Roy," in which Fergus' murder is attributed to the jealousy of Ailill.

Aislinge Oengusso, "The Vision of Angus Óg," is a tale probably dating from the eighth century. The legend, as it is translated by Edward Muller, begins abruptly: "Oengus was sleeping one night when he saw something [like] a maiden near him at the top of his bed."[35] The story as related by Stephens begins with explanatory notes on the god's genealogy and references to the birds associated with him. In Stephens' version, Angus is awake when the vision appears, and he savours the girl's beauty for two pages of ecstatic narration.

In the legend, the vision returns the next night with a lute and plays for Angus, and thus a whole year passes during which she visits him nightly. Stephens shortens the period to one night, but he increases the effect of the vision on the young god so that it is possible to suggest that he falls into a wasting sickness after one visitation. In both the legend and Stephens' tale, several physicians are summoned to diagnose the illness but it is only one, Fergne, who is able to discover the cause as "an accidental love." Stephens also adds a good bit of comic material to what originally were very terse dialogues between Fergne and Angus, Fergne and Boann, and Boann and Angus in *Aislinge Oengusso*.

In the saga, another year elapses as a search is made to locate the girl in Ireland, and it is only after two years that emissaries are sent to Bove, King of the *Shí* of Munster, to solicit his aid. He is given a year to determine the facts, and after a year, locates the girl, and takes Angus to see her. In Stephens' version, the search is made by Fergne, Boann, and Angus, who review daily a parade of the most beautiful women of Ireland by means of visions called up by Angus' father. Stephens seizes this opportunity to display his descriptive skills and his humor, for the project brings delight to Fergne and boredom and depression to Boann. In the saga, it is Ailill who speaks to the girl's father, and it is his household troops who capture Ethal Anbual. Ethal Anbual refuses to give his daughter to Angus because she has greater magical powers than he, for she is able to change to the shape of a bird every other year. In Stephens' rendition, it is Maeve who not only tells the tale but who deals with Fergne and Bove, and it is Maeve who speaks with Ethal Anbual. Further, Maeve, who is hardly timid about her beauty, tells her audience that Fergne found her more beautiful than the daughter of Ethal Anbual. She is the one who sacks the fort, taking with her the whitehorn and brown bulls and bringing on the enmity of the *Shí*, and she argues with Ethal Anbual that his daughter must desire Angus because the girl has presented herself to him in a vision.

In a letter to W. T. H. Howe dated 5 February 1924, Stephens writes: "I am so glad you like 'Deirdre,' but the one I have just finished, 'Etain,' has poor Deirdre licked to the ropes."[36] And again in a letter dated 29 May, Stephens happily tells Howe about his new novel: "it's a corker, at least the second half of it is. Mary Pickford is seconded as the World's Sweetheart. I have her licked to a frazzle with Etain. By George, thats a real girl and she's nicer than pie. She'll make this whole male generation mad that they didnt live two thousand years ago."[37]

Actually Stephens was working with three tales concerning Etain which appear in The Book of the Dun Cow and The Yellow Book of Lecan: the story of Angus Mac Óg, Midir, Etain, and Fuamnach; the story of Etain, Eochaid, and Ailill; and the tale of the chess game played by Midir with Eochaid in order to win back Etain. These stories are included in the Ulster saga because Eochaid Airem, Etain's earthly husband who is also Maeve's uncle, was High King of Ireland at the time of the war between Connacht and Ulster. In "The Feast of Lugnasa," Maeve tells the Etain story, connecting her uncle's sack of the *Shí* of Midir with her own sack of the *Shí* of Ethal Anbual.

According to the first tale, Angus Óg was sent to Midir, King of the *Shí* of Connacht, to be under his tutelage. When Maeve explains to the company that the relationship between Midir and Angus, the love of a man for his foster son, is a deep bond, one is reminded of the beginning of Stephens' tale, "The Wooing of Becfola," which tells of the relationship between King Dermod and his foster son Crimthann. The stories of Etain and Becfola have certain interesting similarities: both women move in the worlds of life and of the *Shí* with equal ease. Etain lives at Tara with Eochaid, but she returns to the *Shí* of Connacht with Midir. Becfola lives with Dermod and Crimthann at Tara, but she is wooed by Flann while in the *Shí*, and she returns there to her lover. Both Midir and Dermod marry beautiful women upon seeing them, and both are betrayed by their wives and their foster sons; in Midir's case, the matter is even more complicated because he has two wives who betray him. After Etain, his second wife, leaves Midir's palace with Angus, she is turned into an insect by a druid at the command of Midir's first wife, Fuam-nach. As such, she is blown into the house of Etar where she falls into a cup of wine and is swallowed by Etar's wife, to be thus reborn as the daughter of Etar in much the fashion of Tuan's rebirth when, in the shape of a fish, he is eaten by the King's wife.

The second tale recounts how Eochaid Airem, King of Ire-land, is faced with a rebellion among his nobles who refuse to come to court until he marries. He finally agrees and sends messengers around the countryside seeking the most beautiful woman of the country, but he finds his own queen when he sees Etain.

In discussing *In the Land of Youth*, Dorothy Hoare[38] argues that "natural affinities by temperament with the matter he deals with" allows Stephens to interpolate material into the story of Nera's adventures and to bring out the humor in the tale of Angus' vision, but she feels that he fails in telling the Eochaid-Etain story, for he spends too much time on Etain's transmigration and makes too pretty a tale of love between Etain and Eochaid. The love between the two *is* idyllic; they play like children until Eochaid's brother, Ailill, falls ill of love for Etain, a disease apparently similar to that suffered by Angus. Etain cures Ailill by agreeing to meet him at night, but when she waits for him it is Midir who appears and tries to woo her back. She does not want to leave Eochaid even when Midir sings the song of bells, a song of the Land of Youth.

In the third tale of Etain, Midir returns disguised as a stranger who challenges Eochaid to a game of chess. He wins the second game, and claims Etain as his prize. He returns the next morn-ing, singing his song, to take her away. Although Stephens reproduces the plot of the first two stories of Etain fairly faith-fully, he shortens this third tale to omit a primitive ending. In the saga, some time after Midir carries Etain away, Eochaid razes Midir's *Shí*, but when Midir defies Eochaid to pick Etain out from the other women of the *Shí*, he selects a woman resembling her who turns out to be Etain's daughter. Eochaid subsequently has a child by this woman.

In the Land of Youth ends rather abruptly after the departure of Etain and Midir with the author's explanation that the book is an "Introduction to the Great Táin." As such, it complements the story in *Deirdre*, not only by expanding the characters of Maeve, Ailill, and Fergus, but by bringing in the object of the Cattle Raid, the dun bull. Although Maeve does not appear at the end of the book, she is asked at the closing of "The Feast of Samhain" about the two bulls she has captured in the *Shí* of Ethal Anbual, and she replies that while the whitehorn is still in Connacht, the dun one has wandered to Ulster. Thus Stephens looks forward to his projected story of the disastrous cattle raid in which Maeve sets out to recover the missing bull.

But Stephens' *Táin* was never completed; he discontinued the project after the publication of *Deirdre* and *In the Land of Youth*. The task was overwhelming, the work exhausting, the critical response to his fifth novel discouraging, and he became too ill in mind and body to continue with the work.

4 Make it Sing/Make it New

A letter to a friend written in 1913 sets forth Stephens' hopes for his poetry:

> ... I have just written a lyric which satisfies me mightily, I enclose a copy as I fancy it will please you also. I am prepared to bet that my poems will be more appreciated ten years hence than my prose. At present they have got overlaid by the Charwoman & the Crock.[1]

It is debatable whether Stephens was correct in his prediction. There are those who identify him as an important Irish poet, but many others find his poetry cloying, dull, dated. As Randall Jarrell has noted, "no one calls James Stephens great, and he long ago stopped being fashionable"; it is only fair, however, to complete Jarrell's remark, "but at his best he is a fine poet."[2] Stephens' poetry, taken as a whole, is clearly not equal to that of his contemporary, Yeats, but if his individual poems are examined, many emerge as memorable and artistic.

INSURRECTIONS (1909)

Stephens filled the earliest volume of his poetry, *Insurrections*, with bold, angry pictures of the Dublin slums and their inhabitants. In these poems garbage is "thick as blood," houses are black with soot, slum dwellers are "grim, noiseless things." This view of city life stands in marked contrast to the sweet innocence, the cheerful aspects, the sustaining camaraderie of *The Charwoman's Daughter*. Here one finds the old and the young cursing their enemies and their circumstances, a beaten down cabdriver, an exhausted clerk, a weary prostitute, a violent tramp. Life is harsh; violence and death are ever present.

Stephens admitted to one of his literary sources when he wrote Lord Dunsany (Edward Plunkett) in 1910 that he believed his verse and Dunsany's prose to be "seeking the same thing, great windy reaches, & wild flights among stars & a very youthful laughter at the gods."[3] In an earlier letter he expressed his admiration for the exotic qualities in Dunsany's stories and said he had attempted to achieve a similar quality in his poetry.[4] Another closer source was Robert Browning, from whom he learned the technique of the dramatic monologue and its use as a means to reveal the eccentric, the striking, or the abnormal character reacting to a stressful situation. By his testimony, Stephens began writing poems after reading the Victorian poet for the first time. Yet having admitted this artistic debt, Stephens still gave himself credit for some of his better works:

> I mentioned that the impulse to write came to me after reading Browning, and I am sure that in Insurrections a certain amount of the Browning method will be discovered, but a great deal is my own — I did not get what Tomas Said in a Pub from him, nor Chill of the Eve, nor the Tale of Mad Brigid, nor Hate and some others, and those which I did get are not among the best things in the book, which does contain poems that I shall never beat.[5]

In one of the most original of the poems, "The Red-Haired Man's Wife," marriage and independence are examined from the standpoint of a woman. Although undoubtedly the poem owes something to Browning in its technique and to Cynthia Stephens in its viewpoint, Stephens has produced a work which remains modern and fresh in its feminist concerns:

I have taken that vow —
  And you were my friend
But yesterday — now
  All that's at an end,
And you are my husband, and claim me, and I
  must depend.

Yesterday I was free,
  Now you, as I stand,
Walk over to me
  And take hold of my hand.
You look at my lips, your eyes are too bold,
  your smile is too bland.

My old name is lost,
  My distinction of race:
Now the line has been crossed,
  Must I step to your pace?
Must I walk as you list, and obey, and smile up
  in your face?

* * * * * * * * * * * * * * * * * *

O, if kneeling were right,
  I should kneel nor be sad,
And abase in your sight
  All the pride that I had,
I should come to you, hold to you, cling to you,
  call to you, glad.

If not, I shall know,
  I shall surely find out,
And your world will throw
  In disaster and rout;
I am woman and glory and beauty, I mystery,
  terror, and doubt.

I am separate still,
  I am I and not you:
And my mind and my will,
  As in secret they grew,
Still are secret, unreached and untouched and
  not subject to you.[6]

"The Dancer" expresses even greater independence of spirit. Told that she must perform before a pub audience of "booted hogs," a young woman refuses:

> I will not dance!
> I say I will not dance.
> Your audience, pah, let them
>   go home again,
> Sleek, ugly pigs. Am I to hop and prance
> As long as they will pay,
> And posture for their eyes, and lay
> My womanhood before them? Let
>   them drain
> Their porter pots and snuffle — I'll
>   not stay.[7]

The punctuation marks beat out a dance of anger; her lover has died and she will stay home to mourn him, whatever the cost of her decision. These two portraits of indignant young women are placed in juxtaposition to those of two older, broken women: Bessie Bobtail, a woman who seems to represent the last stages in the life of old Mrs. Hannigan, continues to walk the roads because she has no place to sit down; her city counterpart, a whore with "old, bad eyes," anxiously trails a prospective customer through the rainy streets.

Throughout the volume there are representations of sexual combat. While the young bride resents her husband's invasion of her privacy, the bride in "The Watcher" faces a more dramatic moment, abduction by a former lover. The dancer quarrels with her audience in coarse terms; the female and male figures seated on ivory thrones in "Nucleolus" are more decorous in language, but just as estranged; the battle is more brutal in "Fossils." Women are fiercely independent here; they need to be to deal with men who are self-satisfied, drunken "clowns" or "pigs." Only "Slán Leath," a poem marking the beginning of the long, enduring relationship between Cynthia and James Stephens holds out the hope for a true marriage of the Contraries.

Other poems, "What Tomas an Buile Said in a Pub" and "The Whisperer," for example, turn from strained human relationships to a search for God's essence and the meaning behind

existence. In some of the poems — certainly in "Bessie Bobtail" — the poet rebels: if "God knows," as Bessie Bobtail
thinks, He is not revealing His thoughts to Stephens. The end
result of the poet's uncertainty is to reject conventional religious
belief and to retreat into nature or into childhood. In sharp
contrast to violent poems such as "The Dancer,""A Street,"
"Where the Demons Grin," and "The Tale of Mad Brigid"
stand the lyrical evocations of nature and love entitled "The
Shell," "Chill of the Eve," and "Slán Leath." "Seumas Beg"
makes his first appearance in this volume as well, bringing
a child's viewpoint which Stephens would present throughout
his writings.

SEUMAS BEG / ROCKY ROAD (1915)

Although some of its poems were written in the same period
as those in *Insurrections*, *The Adventures of Seumas Beg / The Rocky
Road to Dublin* represents a major shift in subject matter
and tone from those vigorous portraits of life's cruelties. Engaging young spirits are apparent in "The Canal Bank" and
"By Ana Liffey." A profoundly patriotic sentiment finds its
way into "York Street," "Dublin Men," "The College of
Science," and other poems which are reminiscent of the fervent
statements contained in essays written for *Sinn Féin*. Among
the last to be composed, the poems describing familiar settings,
for example, Grafton and York Streets, Westland Row, and
O'Connell Bridge, have the bright colors and humming sounds
of the city scenes in *The Charwoman's Daughter*. When the poems
which Stephens called "Dublin sketches" were being composed,
he was in Paris; to make certain that his details were correct,
he wrote to Thomas Bodkin asking him to "recollect any small
street facts."[8] The request recalls that of a fellow exile, James
Joyce, who asked his aunt Josephine Murray for details he
later used in the Ithaca and Penelope sections of *Ulysses*.

Stephens worried over the reception given this volume of
poetry. The reviews were not promising, and although it was
not a collection of children's poems, its title confused librarians
and discouraged prospective readers (as *Irish Fairy Tales* did
later). Perhaps it was unwise to emphasize "Seumas Beg"
(Little James); it gave the critics a chance to complain about
his coy pictures of a young boy whose name linked him directly

to his creator.[9] But if there are sections of arch commentary on childhood here, they are at least made original by the addition of striking portraits of devils, tormented men, and doomed women.

While the *Seumas Beg* poems described the terrors and joys of an imaginative young boy, works in *The Rocky Road* are aphoristic in tone, owing much to the writings of Blake:

> Who knows a thing and will not tell
> Shall spend eternity in hell;
> But he who learns and teaches free
> In heaven spends eternity.[10]

> When a Dublin man shall say
> "Give me a little bread, I pray,"
> If you do not give him bread
> You will be hungry when he is fed.

> And let no priest or magistrate
> Scowl upon the poor man's plate
> Asking him the question sly
> To which no one can reply.[11]

Ironically, one of the best-known pieces in the book is of interest more for its remarkable literary history than for its artistic qualities. "Stephen's Green" is a short poem in which a stiff wind, personified as a wild, mad man, shouts, whistles, kicks, and threatens murder. Stephens liked his work well enough to send it to his friend James Joyce in 1932. Joyce, in turn, liked the poem well enough to translate it into German, Latin, Norwegian, Italian, and French, and then to ask Stephens to add an Irish version so as "to make a rainbow." He even proposed publishing the poem in its many linguistic colors in a pamphlet for "our jubilee year."[12] Stephens was impressed and delighted with Joyce's linguistic accomplishments, but had to admit that he could not translate the poem. "I know English and no more. I tried to break into Irish and French, but got not much further than the front-door-mat in either."[13]

THE HILL OF VISION (1912)

Completed in a period of intense productivity for the writer, *The Hill of Vision* holds works which demonstrate new poetic

influences but also familiar, frequently-repeated subjects
and themes. "A Prelude and a Song" is a good example;
it finds its original sources in Spenser (the "Epithalamion"
to be exact), but it recalls *The Charwoman's Daughter* and *The
Crock of Gold* in its recording of the delights of nature. The
poet expresses his joy in terms of the senses; he delights, as
the Philosopher does after his meeting with Caitilin and Pan,
in the songs of birds, the warmth of the sun, the wind at
play. He sees the milkmaids and satyrs at play, a scene repeated
in the second novel with the shepherdess and the Greek god.
His philosophy is one shared with Pan:

> Good and bad and right and wrong,
> Wave the silly words away:
>
> * * * *
>
> Nor ever question, does the sinner sin?[14]

For the moment Stephens has stopped searching for meaning.
In his delight in earthly pleasures and his love for the creatures
who dance in the sunshine he has allied himself with Pan
in thought and mood. He has not permanently set aside the
question of why there is evil in a world created by God, however,
and he returns to this problem again and again in works of
his middle and later periods. For now he is prepared to embrace
life — but with one qualification. In "Everything That I Can
Spy," "To the Tree," and "Hail and Farewell," we learn
(as we do in *The Crock of Gold*) that the senses are not to
be celebrated by themselves. "A brain to gather the tale
and bless / The prophet who spoke to the wilderness" is requi-
site.

Several poems in *The Hill of Vision* follow the same paths
of works in *Insurrections*. "What the Devil Said" and "Bessie
Bobtail" describe murder, desolation, and madness. Two
poems, "The Tinker's Brat" and "Nothing at All," display
in graphic terms the effects of poverty on human beings;
this is a theme which occupied Stephens throughout his life.
Outrage, fury, and blasphemy are commingled with humor
in "The Sootherer," "Why Tomas Cam Was Grumpy," and
"The Monkey's Cousin."

The best poems in this collection convey rustic joys through simple rhyme schemes, regular metres, plain language, and repetition — not unusual poetic devices, but Stephens adds to them a distinctive whimsical touch. Stanzas from "In the Poppy Field" and "Danny Murphy" may serve as examples:

> Mad Patsy, he said to me,
> That every morning he could see
> An angel walking on the sky:
> Across the sunny skies of morn
> He threw great handfuls far and nigh
> Of poppy seed among the corn;
> And then, he said, the angels run
> To see the poppies in the sun.[15]

> He was as old as old could be,
> His little eye could scarcely see
> His mouth was sunken in between,
> His nose and chin, and he was lean
> And twisted up and withered quite,
> So that he could not walk aright.[16]

There is a wild and an energetic gaiety in the Irish country people portrayed here, not unlike that which John Synge found on the Aran Islands. These poems have a fresh aspect not present in their companion works which employ tired, over-worked personifications: Song as the poet's sister, Misery as a woeful woman, Earth as Mother, and others.

Several poems recall "The Red-Haired Man's Wife" and "Fossils" with their explorations of female-male relationships. "Light-O'-Love" suggests adultery, and "Afterwards" is a monologue spoken by a bride who finds herself "no longer free." In "Nora Criona" a woman whose last name is ironic because it means "the shrewd," pries into her lover's secrets so forcefully that she finds her throat cut. A more appealing work in this vein is a short, charming piece entitled "Wind and Tree," which is known today by its first line, "A woman is a branchy tree." Its message is wry enough to come from Dorothy Parker: a man — like the wind — takes what he wishes from a woman — a branchy tree — until the woman grows older and becomes "a withered woman, a withered tree." He then moves on "undismayed," to "another tree, another maid." One of Stephens' favorite poems, with a long publication history indicative of his affection for it, it began as a section within a long work entitled, "Oisín and Niamh," which was published in *Sinn Féin* in 1910; it next appeared in *The Hill of Vision*; then it was printed in *Collected Poems* under the title "A Woman is a Branchy Tree"; and finally it was published in *The Golden Book Magazine* in 1932 under the title "Wind and Tree."

Despite several memorable poems, *The Hill of Vision* finds Stephens still in his apprenticeship. Even in the most carefully-wrought poems, he occasionally stumbles and uses an inelegant phrase or word. In "A Prelude and a Song" the ear is troubled by "sad vagaries that make us weep," a hair ribbon being "soused" in a brook, "exceeding jollity," "happy minions," "ye sing and hold carouse." Serious subject matter can also cause problems for the poet. Some of the solemn works in *The Hill of Vision* are ponderous and eminently forgettable, "Said the Young-Young Man . . . ," "Treason," "The Lonely God," and "Chopin's Funeral March," for example. And while there are poems happy in their description of life's pleasures, there are also "philosophical" ones which are dreary. Stephens rejected several when preparing for the third edition of this volume, including "Poles," "Mount Derision," "The Spalpeen," and "New Pinions," but the Blakean excesses in this volume are only exceeded by those in *Songs from the Clay.*

SONGS FROM THE CLAY (1915)

According to Stephens his first mentors in the field of poetry were Blake and Browning. If his claim that after reading two books by these artists he wrote twenty-five poems should be dismissed, or at least viewed with a certain indulgent scepticism, it is equally true that his writing from its earliest period to the mature works of the 1920s displays his devotion to Blake.[17] Blake's works gave Stephens a philosophical foundation from which to build his own beliefs, as well as a vocabulary and symbolic system for expressing these concepts. With Blake Stephens insists on the triumph of imagination over reason, emotions, and the merely sensual; he also believes in the wisdom of children, who are the repositories of pure imagination. Where

he parts company with his literary mentor is on the subject
of the deity. Stephens' God is not as powerful — indeed, not
as divine — as Blake's. Instead, Stephens offers a lonely, immo-
bile, "nodding" divinity.

One of his first poems, "The Rivals," has its beginnings
in Blake's *Songs of Innocence*.[18] Other poems, most particularly
"A Street" and "Teig Gorabh and the Liar," reveal the influence of Blake's *Songs* while remaining faithful to Stephens'
own diction and thought. Wordsworth, Shelley, Keats, and
other poets of the Romantic period also served as Stephens'
teachers, strengthening his belief in the uncorrupted state of
childhood, his sentimental view of the poet in solitary contempla-
tion, his love of "unimproved" nature, and his sympathy for
rural inhabitants. Certain, familiar, pastoral symbols drawn
from the Romantic poets and from earlier figures such as Spenser
and Milton pervade Stephens' poetry in this period, for example,
oaten pipes, wreaths of flowers, and rustic figures. His poetic
writing starting around 1912 bears the direct influence of the
Romantic poets almost to the point of direct quotation, certainly
to the imitation of metre, diction, and tone. The poems in
Green Branches, for example, owe much to "Adonais" and its
predecessor "Lycidas," to "Dejection: An Ode," and to "Inti-
mations of Immortality." Some of Stephens' friends were distressed by his poetic dependence. C. P. Curan wrote Alan
Denson that he and others had noticed a difference in Stephens'
writings. Compared to the earthly realism of earlier poems,
those included in *The Hill of Vision* seemed unoriginal, too
derivative, particularly of Blake. ". . . Blake's influence is evident
in *The Hill of Vision*. This book appeared to me in 1912
to be apprentice work and no notable advance on his first
work . . . ."[19]

Stephens was aware that he was being imitative. He wrote
to Edward Marsh and Ralph Hodgson thanking them for a
"devil of a letter" criticizing the manuscript of *Songs from
the Clay* and promising to "retrench certain of these poems,
the Blakeish ones."[20] He wrote Sir Frederick Macmillan, asking
for a delay in publication of the book for a period of time
on the basis of AE's criticism of the manuscript; and he confessed
after the book's publication in 1915 that it was "not nearly
as good as the Hill of Vision."[21]

Ironically, after acknowledging to Edward Marsh that his

poems were "Blakeish," Stephens succumbed to another influence which came to him via Marsh. When he wrote *Insurrections*,
he rejected the Edwardians; now he fell under the influence
of the Georgians, not only providing works for three of Marsh's
anthologies, *Georgian Poetry*, but writing poems filled with the
bland messages, imprecise diction, vague shapes, and uninterest-
ing metrical schemes found in the worst writings of this school.
Even after revision, many of the poems in *Songs* lacked shape
and focus; at best they were graceful, decorative, and charming.
He was not ready to reject the book in its entirety, however:
". . . there are good things in it, & its temper is quite different
from the other book. On the whole I think I like it."[22]

When looking at *Songs from the Clay*, it is particularly interesting to know what Stephens thought were his "best" poems.
In a copy of the book sent to Howe, Stephens commended
the following: "The Rivals," "The Messenger," "Washed in
Silver," "The Voice of God," "The Centaurs," "The Snare,"
"Blue Stars and Gold," "The Nodding Stars," and "Irony."[23]
Stephens' choices center around favorite subjects — bees, clouds,
grass, rabbits — and upon the reciprocal relationship between
the poet and nature: the bees carry messages to the poet's
beloved, the poet sings a psalm to a beautiful sky, a bird
is viewed as a rival, and the stars are lost brothers. Colors
abound; blue stars and gold, grey skies, hills gleaming in silver,
a ruddy setting sun, a pale winter sun, a moon's white circle.
Only "Irony" is a "Blakeish," poem, an awkwardly-told parable
in which a man predicates his belief in a Supreme Being on
God's throwing down a bag of gold. He receives instead "a
broken head," caused by a blow from a bag of lead. Another
favorite, often found in anthologies, employs an unusual
personification in a title which remains unexplained until near
the end of the poem; in "The Fur Coat," an imperious critic
of nature turns out to be a cat, an indolent creature sunning
itself.

When Stephens considered the poems from *Songs* for inclusion
in his collected poetry, he was ruthlessly objective. Comments
on the poems in another copy of the book sent to Howe in
1925 range from "delete," "no good," and "this one is fudge"
to notations about reworkings. "Independence," he admits,
"rather echoes"; "The Twins" is dismissed as "facile," "The
Crown of Thorns" and "The King of the Fairy Men" are

"too easy."[24] These poems are poor imitations of Blake, and they, along with the others which he eliminated, deserve their fate.

By 1915, work on *Songs* and *Seumas Beg*, the war in Europe, and the ever present struggle to make a living for his family had depressed Stephens. In October he wrote Edward Marsh that his "poetry shop" was closing, claiming that the *Seumas Beg* poems made "a decent 'good-bye' to the craft."[25] Perhaps he was also worried over AE's comment on *Songs*, that there was not "the same full chord of feeling" in it which the reader found in the earlier books of poetry. "It is not that you as a writer are losing power but you are putting your increasing power into other work. To write verse as good as your other things you would have to stop prose I think."[26] This was not AE's first complaint about the change in Stephens' poetry. Although he praised *Insurrections* for its energy, unorthodox beauty, and "unfeigned humanity," he found less satisfaction with *The Hill of Vision*, confessing that he preferred Stephens' "tinker drunken to his Deity sober." But Stephens did not close his shop; he continued to write poetry until the completion of his last book, *Kings and the Moon*.

GREEN BRANCHES (1916)

Green Branches consists of three poems — "Autumn 1915," "Spring 1916," and "Joy Be With Us" — published in memory of the Easter Rising and its martyred heroes. The first piece begins an examination of the seasons, starting with the world of summer, a fair, free, beautiful time, and moving toward the autumn in which the sap is ebbing away from "the great tree." The tree, at once both a reference to the Tree of Life and to humankind, can no longer be considered immortal; it will disappear along with the poet and his audience when winter comes and the year dies. Stephens pictures himself here, a "saddened elf" no longer playing his reed, wandering in the hills, seeking solace in nature from the harsh truths of reality. "Spring 1916" completes the cycle of seasons, bringing death (the execution of the leaders of the rebellion) and renewal (the bringing of a new national spirit to the Irish people and a new sense of purpose to the poet). In this poem the great tree again is green, a particularly appropriate image because of the "four green fields," Ireland.

The despair which accompanied "Autumn 1915" has been replaced by purposeful action; there are flowers to be gathered, garlands to be woven for those who died for Ireland. The greening tree will provide the branches to lay upon the graves of the martyrs, much as Parnell's coffin was draped with ivy. This poem serves as Stephens' gift, a green branch to be laid with the others at the feet of the fallen heroes. Thus all honor the heroes: the poet, the tree, even Spring offers fragrant buds, the sound of birds, and the beauty of "newly-greening earth." In "Joy Be With Us," the sonnet which ends the sequence, the Irish respond to nature and look forward with hope. At the end of the poem, Ireland is mentioned by name and personified as a woman who triumphantly sets sail with Mananán, the Irish god of the sea. Thus begins an adventure as affirmative and symbolic as the union of Caitilin and Angus Óg. The note of optimism on which the poem ends stands in marked contrast to the elegies written by Yeats and others for the Easter Uprising. This mood of reconciliation recalls the ending lines of *The Insurrection in Dublin*, "From this day the great adventure opens for Ireland."

REINCARNATIONS (1918)

In June 1917, after a period of inactivity brought on by the Troubles in Ireland and abroad, Stephens wrote Edward Marsh:

> I had not been flourishing since the war began until the 1st of this month when I began to flourish like a whole nursery of green bay trees. . . . One night I wrote nine poems. If I keep on I will get back to my old form of 15 poems between dark & dawn.[27]

The poems were part of those included in *Reincarnations* (1918). This collection, based on works written by Irish poets of the seventeenth and eighteenth centuries, is the beginning point of an exploration of Gaelic materials which culminates in *Irish Fairy Tales*, *Deirdre*, and *In the Land of Youth*. The title of the collection reflects the fact that the poems are not Stephens'

translations but rather new forms of old works.[28] Stephens could
speak Gaelic, but not fluently; he could write the language
in simple sentences, but not without misspelling words; and
he could read Irish but only with the help of a dictionary.
His friends and acquaintances included the translators and poets
Osborn Bergin, Douglas Hyde, and Stephen MacKenna, for-
tunately. He found the original version of some of his adaptations
in Hyde's *The Love Songs of Connacht* and *Songs Ascribed to Raftery*;
those poems based on the works of Egan O'Rahilly and David
O'Bruadair are reworkings of originals translated in the editions
of Patrick S. Dinneen, S. J., and Tadhg O'Donoghue and
John MacErlean, S. J.[29]

Stephens' version of "The Coolun," a poem he ascribes to
Raftery, is instructive of his method of adaptation. The poem,
as translated by Hyde, is a sixteen line work:

A honey mist on a day of frost, in a dark oak wood,
And love for thee in the heart of me, thou bright,
    white, and good;
Thy slender form soft and warm, thy red lips apart,
Thou has found me, and hast bound me, and put
    grief in my heart.

In fair-green and market, men mark thee, bright, young,
    and merry.
Though thou hurt them like foes with the rose of thy blush
    of the berry;
Her cheeks are a poppy, her eye it is Cupid's helper,
But each foolish man dreams that its beams for himself are.

Whoe'er saw the Coolun in a cool dewy meadow
On a morning in summer in sunshine and shadow;
All the young men go wild for her, my childeen, my treasure,
But now let them go mope, they've no hope to possess her.

Let us roam, O my darling, afar through the mountains,
Drink milk of the goat, wine and bulcán in fountains;
With music and play everyday from my lyre,
And leave to come rest on my breast when you tire.[30]

Stephens has created his twenty-line version out of the fourth stanza, concentrating on the lover's invitation rather than the description of the young girl:

> Come with me, under my coat,
>   And we will drink our fill
> Of the milk of the white goat,
>   Or wine if it be thy will;
>   And we will talk until
> Talk is a trouble, too,
>   Out on the side of the hill,
> And nothing is left to do,
>   But an eye to look into an eye
> And a hand in a hand to slip,
>   And a sigh to answer a sigh,
> And a lip to find out a lip:
>   What if the night be black
> And the air on the mountain chill,
>   Where the goat lies down in her track
> And all but the fern is still!
>   Stay with me, under my coat,
> And we will drink our fill
>   Of the milk of the white goat
> Out on the side of the hill.[31]

He has eliminated the internal rhyme, replacing it with repetition: "talk," "eye," "hand," "sigh," "lip" are words used twice in close proximity. He has reduced the references to "honey mist," "dark wood," "red lips," "fair-green," etc.; the only colors now are black and white. By paring down the nonessential, by repeating simple words and phrases, and by increasing the use of connectives, he creates a poem which has an incantatory effect. Clearly it is an irresistible invitation to love.

In "Mary Hynes," a reworking of the third stanza of a poem by Raftery, he again relies on repetition, simple diction and construction, and compression of thought to produce an extraordinarily beautiful, lyrical recreation. The words of the poem describe the work itself: "airy," "lovely," "good." Stephens often works in this fashion, cutting down his source and building his adaptation on a few phrases, but he may retain or even elaborate upon certain images which he finds in his sources. A reference to Nancy Walsh's "ringleted" hair in Raftery's six-stanza poem remains in Stephens' much shorter version. The first two stanzas of "Peggy Mitchell" are an expansion of Raftery's phrase "as the foliage and blossoms rise." Raftery's six-stanza lament on the death of Anthony O'Daly is reduced to one stanza, but what is "reincarnated" is very similar in wording to Raftery's fourth stanza. "Eileen, Diarmuid and Teig," a reworking of O'Rahilly's "On the Death of Tadhg O'Cronin's Three Children," retains O'Rahilly's repetition of the word "three," his imagery, and much of his language, but it is a much shorter poem in which the Gaelic poet's introduction to the legend and his traditional verses on mourning are omitted. "Inis Fál" is built upon two lines of "The Wounds of the Land of Fodla," a lament for an earlier time in which, O'Rahilly says, the Gaels had "charity, hospitality, manners, and sweet music." Stephens expands upon these qualities while eliminating the Gaelic poet's appeal for divine assistance. He also follows closely his source for "Odell," a poem by O'Bruadair, but adds a contemporary example, Germany, to the poet's complaint that the Irish often find themselves fighting against their potential allies.

For Stephens, O'Bruadair was "one of the most interesting, tormented, angry and eloquent bards I have met with," a "georgeous, a very learned man and a very poor one, a man who was devout and thirsty in equal and terrific extreme."[32] He sympathized with this poet's rage over society's neglect, and he delighted in O'Bruadair's curse, "Once an Insolent, Vindictive, Lank, and Shrivelled Servant Girl," which he adapted as "Righteous Anger." His version contains much of O'Bruadair's wording, but he has rearranged the order of the original lines and neglected to change his last line, a wish that the girl develop the mange and give birth to a cat, which was based on an incorrect rendering of the Irish and English translation of the poem made and then revised by John MacErlean.

Stephens' adaptations are based on structural aspects of Irish poetry which he has modified to fit a modern audience. From the thirteenth to the seventeenth centuries, the bards, Ireland's professional poets, maintained special schools for instruction in the writing of poetry so that poems might be composed under strict metrical rules.[33] Douglas Hyde has provided an example of a bardic form called *Séadna* as it would appear in English translation:

> Teig of herds the gallant giver,
> Right receiver of our love,
> Teig thy name shall know no ending
> Branch un-bending, Erin's glove.[34]

Lines *b* and *d* rhyme, the final of line *c* rhymes with the stressed word preceding the final words of line *d*; there are internal rhymes and alliteration; and the lines alternate in length of syllables. Hyde's verse follows the rules but it is hardly lyrical. Stephens succeeds better in his efforts to capture the bardic tradition in these lines adapted from a poem by Geoffrey Keating, a writer of the seventeenth century:

> O woman full of wiliness!
> Although for love of me you pine,
> Withhold your hand adventurous
> It holdeth nothing holding mine.[35]

He does not alternate the number of syllables in his lines, but he does combine assonance, alliteration, and rhyme.

By the eighteenth century Gaelic poetry was much freer in form. Longer metres measured by stress predominated. The works continued to hold interlocked assonance and had a musicality difficult to translate into English. Stephens discovered this in his attempts to translate Raftery's lovely poem "The County Mayo." As he explains to his reader:

> The first three verses are not bad, but the last verse is the completest miss: the simplicity of the original is there, its music is not, and in the last two lines the poignance, which should come on the reader as though a hand gripped at his heart, is absent.[36]

Nevertheless, Stephens' poems not only in *Reincarnations* but elsewhere clearly follow in the Gaelic tradition. In addition to metrical experimentation, there are certain qualities of Irish poetry which are found in abundance in Stephens' work: the presence of epigrammatic speech, epithets, wit, and hyperbole; concrete language and color in descriptive passages: a use of sharp words and curses; many lists of three items, emotions, or actions; impressionistic descriptions of nature or animals; a sense of refuge in the countryside; a lyricism which suggests music conveyed in words; a sentimental feeling toward an Ireland personified as a woman in need of protection; and moods of exuberance and melancholy.

Stephens' selections of works to adapt are interesting because their themes reflect his interests and preoccupations throughout his writing career with the relativity of time and man's mortality, love's manifold forms, beauty both human and in nature, Ireland's place in history, its legends, and the poet and his craft. He chose to work mainly with Raftery, O'Rahilly, and O'Bruadair's poems because they represented aspects of his own work: in Raftery he found a kindred spirit who loved the beauties of nature; in O'Bruadair and O'Rahilly he saw a point of view not unlike his own in their laments over the loss of heroic ideals. In O'Bruadair, particularly, he discovered a man who fought against materialism, foreign domination, and pro-British sentiment. Because of this sympathy in spirit, his adaptations of O'Bruadair's poems often come closer to the originals than his reworking of the other poets.

Viewed as a whole, the poems written by O'Bruadair, O'Rahilly, and Raftery reveal the Irish poet alienated from his society by his rare, artistic gifts, his far-too-discriminating eye, his faithfulness to an aristocratic past, his poverty, or even (despite its leveling quality) his need for drink. The poets' quarrel with their fellow citizens — and it is Stephens' quarrel also — is over the Irish people's lack of appreciation of their own culture and history and their acceptance, instead, of "foreign vulgarity." To fight this unthinking, insensitive world, Stephens sought to recreate O'Bruadair's powerful yet humorous rage, O'Rahilly's graceful beauty, and Raftery's lyrical tenderness, qualities admirably demonstrated in the poems he chose to open the sections of the book devoted to adaptations of poet's works — "Righteous Anger," "Eileen, Diarmuid and Teig," and "Mary Hynes."

LITTLE THINGS (1924)

As small a volume as *Little Things* can be illustrative of Stephens' poetry throughout his career. The six poems in the book encompass his most frequent subjects: animals, emotions, human knowledge, and Ireland. "Little Things" is a prayer to nature's creatures, suggestive of Blake and Burns perhaps, but beautiful in its simplicity. The rhythmic repetition of the word "and," the use of sets of common items and actions, and the artless innocence of diction and rhyme suggest the throbbing heart of a frightened animal. This poem is an example of many beautifully-simple works in which Stephens' sympathy goes out to wounded, fearful, neglected animals and human beings, and in which he attempts to understand man's inhumanity and God's (presumed) indifference.

"The Pit of Bliss" is a complex poem on the joys of knowledge and "singing," owing much to Blake, Shelley, and Wordsworth. "Nachiketas and Death" is a more original attempt at metaphysical thought, looking forward to Stephens' late-period poetry, with its emphasis on man, "the dreamer and the dream," and on Eastern religious belief. Stephens was pleased with the poem as a letter to Howe indicates:

I would like you to read, in particular, "Nachiketas & Death". It is rather a feat to put the whole of the Upanishads & the Vedanta into verse, & to put it so shortly. I might say that it took me fifteen years to write that poem, although I actually did write it in ten minutes.[37]

"Lesbia" and "Green Weeds" deal with love and jealousy in a matter reminiscent of the poems inserted into *Here Are Ladies*.

"On the Freedom of Ireland" moves into the area of the contemporary politics in a subtle, understated manner not unlike the poems in *Green Branches*. The "Irishness" of this poem is so deeply imbedded that at first it seems almost nonexistent. Few references to Ireland can be found in its lines; only the phrases "everything is free," "not for duty," "Thankless, uncomplaining," and "Death, unasked, hath he bestirred" and the poem's dedication to Eamonn de Valera, President of Sinn Féin, suggest the guns and blood of the Irish Civil War in 1922, the date of the first publication of this poem in *Poblacht na h-Eireann*. As the poet and his companions move in a minuette of love and devotion, nature joins them. The moon, the wind, the rose, and a star bring peacefulness to the heart despite the uncertainty of "chancing" things.

MINOR WORKS, 1925–29

Three small volumes each containing one poem were published between 1925 and 1929. *Christmas in Freelands* (1925) was written as a poem to be used by W. T. H. Howe as a Christmas greeting. Stephens typically selected nature as the subject matter:

> I laughed with joy when I got your royal command, & sat right down at the job, saying, if my friend W. T. H. H., wants a poem he is sure going to get one if it bursts every button I've got. I hope Daisy is pleased, but I expect she would say, were she fronted with it, "poem about me! I should worry, I'm a poem myself! Besides", she might continue, "none of these humans can create real poetry, only cows can do that — Bull-cows that is ", she would amend it, & get again to her muncheon.[38]

The poem is a sprightly reminiscence of Freelands, Howe's estate. Its wintry snow, the cow Daisy, and the donkey Stephens rode are linked to the traditional image of the manger, mother, and child; thus past and present, myth and reality, are connected.

The Outcast (1929) is a depiction of Gloom, who complains that he has no place to go, no welcome. The narrator-poet promptly takes Gloom to heart until he can become a "Child of Joy," but by this charitable act the poet becomes "dark" and will remain so until Gloom "Is Joy, and gives Joy back to me." *The Optimist* (1929) is a funny complaint that the poet rarely gets the Muses' inspiration for a "theme that is every poet's dream." Rather, he gets "toys": "Poetic-stuff for little boys, / Love-stuff! Wisdom! That and this!" while Shakespeare, Wordsworth, and Keats have received "his" poetry.

A Poetry Recital, published in June 1925, is a collection of poems Stephens used during his first American speaking tour in 1925.[39] As such, the poems selected were those which could be read aloud with effect, and some are less poems than vocal exercises. The subject matter ranges from animals, mountains, the sea, and flowers to "the passion of love," from experiments in oral interpretation to adaptations of Irish poems taken from *Reincarnations*. "The Main Deep," one of Stephens' favorite poems, demonstrates his attempts at technical experimentation. It is a poem without a verb which concentrates on the description of a wave observed as it gathers speed, then breaks. The poem starts slowly, with two four-syllable lines, then picks up tempo by shifting to three-syllable lines. The lines leading to the climactic moment when the wave breaks contain only two accents; the climax is signaled by an additional accent:

> On — on — on

The final line again holds two accents and is repeated as calm prevails:

> Hush — hushing
> Hush — hushing

In *A Poetry Recital* Stephens also experimented with accented letters of words. As he explained to the reader in a footnote to "His Will":

The letters marked with an accent are to be prolonged as long as it is possible to sound them. Count two beats of that duration at the end of each line, and for the silences between each verse. These sounds and silences are to be considered as one rhythmic utterance.[40]

This remark and the title of the volume suggest that Stephens viewed the reading of poems aloud as an art; indeed as he explained in his BBC talk "On Speaking Verse," he believed that song underlies poetry and that speakers of verse too often use only one voice — and that a monotonous one — when there are adjustments to make in the speaking voice depending upon the kind of poetry being read:

There is a form, generally the epic, which is to be uttered

in a fashion approximating to gravely-modulating speech. There is a form, the lyrical, which, without being sung approximates to singing. And there is an intermediate form which is come to by a subtle balancing of phrase against phrase.[41]

COLLECTED POEMS (1926)

His experiments with poetry as sound continue throughout the 1920s and later; for example, he took older poems and broke long lines into shorter ones, adding exclamation marks, dashes, and dots for emphasis. The first stanza of the version of "The Goat Paths" published in *Songs from the Clay* read:

> The crooked paths go every way
> Upon the hill — they wind about
> Through the heather in and out
> Of the quiet sunniness.
> And there the goats, day after day,
> Stray in sunny quietness,
> Cropping here and cropping there,
> As they pause and turn and pass,
> Now a bit of heather spray,
> Now a mouthful of the grass.[42]

It appeared this way in *Collected Poems*:

> The crooked paths
> Go every way
> Upon the hill
> — They wind about
> Through the heather,
> In and out
> Of a quiet
> Sunniness.
>
> And the goats,
> Day after day,
> Stray
> In sunny
> Quietness;

Cropping here,
And cropping there
— As they pause,
And turn
And pass —
Now a bit
Of heather spray,
Now a mouthful
Of the grass.[43]

The later version marks the beat of the goats' hooves, it moves
as they do, turning, then pausing, then starting again.

Another poem in *Songs from the Clay*, "And It Was Windy
Weather," is broken into stanzas, exclamation marks are added,
and the wording is heightened for dramatic effect before publication in *Collected Poems*:

Now the winds are riding by,
Clouds are galloping the sky,
And the trees are lashing their
Leafy plumes upon the air;
They are crying as they sway —
"*Pull the roots out of the clay,*
Dance away, O, dance away;
Leave the rooted place and speed
To the hill-side and the mead,
To the roaring seas we go,
Chase the airy birds, and know
Flying high, flying high,
All the freedom of the sky,
All the freedom of the sky."[44]

Now the winds are riding by;
Clouds are galloping the sky;

Bush and tree are lashing bare,
Savage, boughs on savage air;

Crying, as they lash and sway,
— Pull the roots out of the clay!

Lift away: away:
Away!

Leave security, and speed
From the root, the mud, the mead!

Into the sea and air we go!
To chase the gull, the moon! — and know,

— Flying high!
Flying high!

All the freedom of the sky!
All the freedom of the sky![45]

As Stephens' preface indicates, the selections in *Collected Poems* have been arranged into six sections by theme, mood, and subject rather than by chronology. With such an arrangement he can group works according to topic, specifically, man's reactions to nature, to women, to the seasons, to the world, to life's difficulties, and finally to life itself. The number three, a recurrent, magical unit in Irish saga materials and first found in Stephens in the sets of stories making up *Here Are Ladies*, dominates the first section of *Collected Poems*, "In Green Ways." In this grouping of poems on man's relationship to nature, time, and space, there are three-part poems and collections of three objects, for example, moon, wind, heart; Beauty, Music, Star. Poems in this section reveal nature's freedom and pain, animals in sunny solitude and entrapped by man's cruel snares. Also included is "Spring 1916," in which green branches mark the return of life to Ireland after the coldness of winter and the deaths caused by the Easter Rebellion. The second section, "A Honeycombe," observes a progression in male-female relationships from the joys of love to hints of trouble, minor altercations, and violent battles. These poems are reflective of Stephens' attitude toward women: feminine power and beauty are celebrated here. "In the Two Lights" is a return to nature with its contrasts of clear skies and storms, Spring's green ways and the etched frosts of winter. Audaciousness, anger, and blasphemy are found in the fourth section "Head and Heels," in works such as "What Tomas Said in a Pub," "The Market," and "Bessie Bobtail," but also there are the delights of childhood, tranquility, and joy. The fifth unit, "Less than Daintily," records anger and societal abuse. Optimism returns in the final section in which the joys of life, love, nature, and music are ever present, and death is countered by rebirth.[46]

Stephens worked hard on the selection of the poems for this book. As he admitted to W. T. H. Howe, he rewrote many of them, altering punctuation, line length, and diction, while looking for ways to present them in sequences and rejecting what could not be saved. Poems he believed to be too obvious in their source were rejected; many of the "Blakeish" poems remaining in the third edition of *The Hill of Vision* and in *Songs from the Clay* were not reprinted. Over thirty works from *Seumas Beg / Rocky Road* were also ignored. Others received changes in title; for example, "Nucleolus" became "The Nucleus," a move away from its Theosophical origins, and "The Satyr" was revised and retitled, "The Crackling Twig," a more decorous title for a less lively poem. The first poem of *Green Branches* was separated from its companion pieces, a decision which only revealed the weakness of the three pieces when they were not viewed as one work; and only four sections of *A Prelude and a Song* were reprinted in scattered fashion which, again, exposed their weakness as isolated poems. The task was not without its comic moments:

I am working at my Collected Poems. Tis a troublesome, but entertaining job; and there are so many poems that it is difficult to make a sequence. I'm trying it in genres & species — A bunch of grotesque-verse, tapering into "ideas"-verse [.] Another swathe of pastoral poems (& jolly good they are!) [—] Then a crowd of verses showing People — Next verses in the Irish mode, & then Thought-verses (the style of your Nachiketas & Death) [—] But verse is a nimble matter — It doesnt stay "put". They lap, & overlap & overflow: They become "grotesques" that has been "pastorals", and, if I may say so, vice-verses. It is, I think, about as easy to organise a Sodality of Fleas, as a book of verse.[47]

LATER POETRY, 1930–38

In the Preface to *Collected Poems*, Stephens draws a number of contrasts between poetry and prose. He holds poetry as a higher act, claiming that lyric poetry is an intensification of life, capable of composition in a wide variety of *tempi* and subjects, whereas prose, at least prose in the modern period, is a "mentally lazy" portrayal of "action for the sake of action." His recommendation to writers of prose is that they study epic poetry, with its subtle blank-verse form, its grave matter, and its "romantic or truth-telling" subject matter.[48] While it is not surprising to find an advocacy of poetry in a preface to a collection of poetry, Stephens continued his defense of the genre in *On Prose and Verse* (1928), claiming that "everything that is in his nature helps the person who can write poetry to write it," and that it intensifies life and never grows stale.[49]

His last three volumes, *Theme and Variations* (1930), *Strict Joy* (1931), and *Kings and the Moon* (1938) contain poems which further explore the subject. One section in *Theme and Variations* proclaims that the poet should be pitied "more than other men":

> . . . his hopes and fears
> Are those same ravening dogs that bay
> The moon, and bury bones in clay!
>
> Tho' he on offals too was bred,
> Tho' in his heart, and in his head
> The brute doth slaver, yet he can
> Banish the brute from off the man,
> The man from that beyond the man.[50]

"Strict Care, Strict Joy" suggests a more affirmative conclusion: the poet's task is to make out of sorrow a thing of beauty. The poverty of O'Bruadair, the blindness of Raftery, the broken heart of O'Rahilly were the bases of their poems, and in turn their poems, being beautiful, transfigured their grief into joy. Stephens resolves that he will also seek to create art out of the ashes of sorrow.

The writing of his books based on the *Táin* followed years

of study; Stephens brought to his later poetry a similar preparation consisting of readings in Eastern philosophy. As early as 1907, he had attended AE's lectures on the *Upanishads* at the Hermetic Society; as late as the 1930s he was studying the *Mahabharata* and making notes on it. He first read the *Mahabharata* in 1913, and in the 1920s he studied the *Upanishads*, the *Vedas*, the *Bhagavadgita*, *The Yoga-Vasishtha-Maharamayana of Valmiki*, and D. T. Suzuki's *Essays in Zen Buddhism*. Many aspects of Buddha's teaching appealed to him, namely, the principles of individual responsibility and freedom of thought, the absence of the doctrine of "sin" and its replacement by the evils of ignorance and false views, the emphasis on knowing rather than believing, the renunciation of power, persecution, greed, and warfare, and the seeking of peace, self-control, goodness, and compassion for all living things. Stephens drew upon the writings of Buddhism for many of his poems, particularly those which revealed his belief in achieving wisdom through annihilation of desire and concentration on knowledge and love.

His utilization of Eastern thought in "Nachiketas and Death" has already been noted. In *Theme and Variations* Stephens combines his knowledge of Eastern philosophy with the conception of Ideal Beauty set forth by Plotinus. Temporal beauty is placed in contrast with the joy of eternal life in Nature, and inspiration leads to all that the universal mind holds. "Sarasvati," the title of a poem in *Strict Joy*, is the name in Hindu literature for the wife of Brahma, the creator-god; she is the goddess of wisdom, eloquence, and learning. Celebrated in her poem are the refuges of love: the bird's nest, the beehive, a mother's arms.

Theme and Variations, which is dedicated to Stephen Mac-Kenna, a friend and translator of Plotinus, consists of a long poem setting forth an introduction, a theme, sixteen variations, and a coda. Stephens takes as his theme, memory as the repository of all sensation and thought. His variations range in tone from humor to terror, they encompass love and murder, and their settings are Spring and Winter. The poems in *Strict Joy* also contain familiar images from nature in its pleasant and dangerous aspects and shifts from gay to solemn mood. The subject matter and tone of both books are not new, then, and their language is only occasionally bolder than the middle period, for example, in these excerpts from *Theme and Variations*:

> The hills shall crumble down, and roll
> Underneath an iron sea!
> And the tropics with the pole
> Shall be frozen equally![51]

> The wing that bears the albatross
> Over the gulf that he would cross
> Is kingly . . .[52]

Personifications abound in the later poems: the Will triumphs over Emotion, Thought, and Imagination; Desire is a "web;" and the Mind is "ignorance, inconstancy." Only a few poems, most notably "Apple Blossom," "The White Swan," and "Cadence," look backward to *The Hill of Vision* in their sweetness and direct expression.

AE's primary role in Stephens' life was that of friend and advocate, but he also served as teacher. Although poems in *The Hill of Vision* owe much to Blake, Stephens' war against untempered reason, his pagan beliefs, his view of Earth as the "great mother," and his occasional, sometimes only inferred visions of an ideal world come from AE. "The Breath of Life" owes its existence to AE's belief in mystical experience brought about by meditation; in "The Lonely God" even the Deity meditates and in the process discovers that he needs to improve his life. Stephens' later poems give in to mysticism, losing sight of land and people in their search for the Will, the Demiurge, or what Stephens calls "That." AE first brought Stephens in contact with the literature of Eastern religions, but if he disliked Stephens' "Deity sober," it is hard to believe that he would have found any pleasure in the poet sober. In the final poems Stephens describes process and doctrine rather than people or emotion, and he posits his beliefs rather than argues his case. What followed from this artistic decision are poems filled with references to abstract qualities — the Good, the Beautiful, the True, Love, Loving, etc. What the poems make clear, unfortunately, is that nothing comes from nothingness.

Poems in *Kings and the Moon* are permeated with their author's mood of depression: they speak of lost love, of the coming of winter, of growing old. The poet ranges from weary dejection

to cold indifference as he contrasts the arid modern times with
the richness of the past. In one of the finest poems in the
collection, "I am Writer," however, Stephens escapes from
his unhappiness into his work and describes the task of a poet
in beautifully simple language:

> I am writer,
> And do know
> Nothing that is false,
> Or true:
>
> Have only care
> To take it so,
> And make it sing,
> And make it new:
>
> And make it new,
> And make it sing,
> When if it's pleasing
> Unto you,
>
> Say, I've done
> A useful thing
> — As your servant
> Ought to do.[53]

This poem, "To Lar, with a Biscuit," "Envying Tobias," "In
the Red," "Student Taper," and "Paternoster" illustrate Lud-
wig Mies van der Rohe's principle "less is more." Stephens'
attempts at complexity do not work — "Titan with Paramour,"
"Or Where Guile Find," and "For the Lion of Judah" are
lifeless — but a few poems, such as "Gathering the Waters,"
"Withdrawn in Gold," and "The Mighty Mother," which
reflect the influence of the Romantics, succeed by their achievement of the qualities Stephens holds dear in those nineteenth-
century poets: inner vitality, intensity, and grace of expression.

THE POETRY IN PERSPECTIVE

If it is viewed in its entirety, Stephens' poetry may be seen
as a progression from an early concentration on the real — nat-

ural rhythms, speech, figures, and situations — to a later search for the ideal — a dispensing of details, a desire to become bodiless, a need to expound, at most a qualified ("Strict") Joy. Blake and Browning were inspirations for the simplicity, purity of thought, and directness of language found throughout his poems; the works of the Romantic Poets, Spenser, and Milton were models for his middle-period of writing; Emerson and AE influenced the last works; Raftery, O'Bruadair, and other Gaelic poets played a role at various points in his development as a poet.

The earliest poetry combines whimsy and coarseness, audacity and simplicity, the grotesque and the profound. An urban childhood is revealed in the harsh reality of poverty always just beneath the surface of his early poems, but the tone is often buoyant, frequently optimistic, always humane even as the subject matter ranges over earth and cosmos. Middle-period poems mirror childhood innocence, mourn the advance of a mechanical age, attack restrictive societal conventions such as law, religion, and government, and record a belief in the union of the Contraries. Those works written at the end of his life are less personal, more opaque in subject matter.

In his recreations of Gaelic poetry in *Reincarnations*, Stephens changes metre and length, alters language, and contracts lengthy exposition to fit a modern audience. His stylistic experimentations are observable, however, from the earliest poems. In the first stanza of "Fifty Pounds a Year and a Pension," alternating line lengths intensify a picture of nature which an impoverished, elderly city clerk will never see. The long fifth line of each stanza in "The Red-Haired Man's Wife" is another example of a heightening of emotion; the woman's feelings of entrapment, rage, then growing power are marked by the contrast in length of this line with the lines which precede it. Works in *Insurrections*, *The Hill of Vision*, and *Songs from the Clay* generally fall into one of two categories: those based on traditional schemes of rhyme and metre and those in which Stephens has varied the schemes for effect. In the first case, his audacious language often provides a striking contrast with the traditional poetic form.

Experimentation with metre continues in the later works in which Stephens presents his philosophical and aesthetic tenets. In *Kings and the Moon*, for example, repeated refrains, irregular rhyme schemes, and shortened lines are used to express the poet's feelings, reactions, and thoughts. The metres are fairly regular, however, if the verse is read aloud in its entirety; for example, the first two verses of "Wild Dove in Wood-Wild" are ten-syllable iambic verse with trochaic first feet:

> Nothing do I withhold,
> And I am fair:
>
> Do not thou,
> Bold,
> Adventure otherwhere:[54]

By putting "Bold" on a separate line, Stephens emphasizes a daring step, "adventuring" elsewhere. Broken metres, where they exist, intensify emotions or emphasize a concept, for example, excitement over the entrance of royalty in "The King." In "Withdrawn in Gold" the variations point up the similarity between the pure mind and the moon and stars: both the mind and the "Shining Ones" may withdraw from the world and thereby shine "in greater splendour." Generally he uses short lines for statements of feelings or belief, as in "Paternoster," and long lines for wrestling with a philosophical problem, as in "Or Where Guile Find."

Oliver Gogarty recalls the days in which Stephens would recite lyrics which he had kept in his head "all day long," saying that he had been sitting on the poems, "keeping them warm like a hen on a nest of eggs." The early poems reveal Stephens' delight in creatures large and small and his ability to "become" the object or person he is describing, whether that is a goat, a mountain, or a milkmaid. Works from his middle-period demonstrate this ability and another characteristic, musicality. Stephens loved to sing — a favorite ballad taught to him by Joyce was "O the brown and the yellow ale" — and his poems reveal his sense of timing, phrasing, pitch, and tone. The later works are removed from the sounds, the sights, the creatures of Ireland. When the spontaneous flow of ideas and images ceased, the poetry became stagnant, the tone world-weary, or, worse, complacent. But there are poems which transcend the *ennui*: "The White Swan," and "Wild Dove in the Wood-Wild" are exquisite, tender love poems, whose imagery and colors link them to earlier works.

What connects Stephens' poetry early and late is the doctrine of correspondences. From his readings in Irish mythology and legend, Blake's prophetic books, Theosophical teachings, and the wisdom recorded in Eastern literature, he draws his belief in a heritage shared by all creatures. This belief in the connections among gods, tramps, animals, and trees, and between the living and the non-living, lightens the darkest moods and extends the impact of his poetry. Thus, we feel the sunshine on the winding goat paths, the coldness of the rain-soaked Dublin streets, the pain of a trapped rabbit. Thus, Deirdre's plight becomes our plight; we experience O'Bruadair's rage; and we share Stephens' wish for angels, his fears of growing old, and his need to be a poet.

5 The Art and Craft of Prose

During the period from 1907 to 1916, Stephens was writing poetry and prose in more or less equal amounts, and his letters to Lord Dunsany, W. T. H. Howe, and Lewis Chase reveal his concern over their development.

> For my part I am hammering out with great labour a prose style. I was enamoured of the purplest patches & used to wave my arms & lips at once, also I used to make jokes that one could both hear & see from a great distance. I am only beginning to get out of these crudities & I really believe I have got a grip on something that is very like a style.[1]

> One can polish a short story just like a poem.[2]

> I wrote prose as I write verse. That is, I scan and pore every line of it, and I do that an hundred times before the "easy" phrase has been evolved. I will say no more on this personal aspect lest you should conclude I was the most egotistic of writers instead of one deeply interested in the art and craft of letters — the blatancy is not personal but crafty[3]

Stephens turned to prose originally because he believed that the torrent of energy contained within a young writer could not be absorbed by composing poetry alone. The short stories, sketches, essays, and book reviews Stephens contributed to Dublin's newspapers between 1907 and 1912 are apprentice work, but they are important demonstrations of his attempts to "hammer out" a literary style. His first piece in print — earlier critical commentaries to the contrary — was not "The Greatest Miracle," a sketch appearing in *The United Irishman* in 1905; that work has subsequently been identified as written by Seumas O'Sullivan. Instead, it was "The Seoinin," a patriotic essay appearing on 20 April 1907 in *Sinn Féin*.

CONTRIBUTIONS TO SINN FÉIN

Eighteen essays in *Sinn Féin* and *Sinn Féin Daily* are in the form of lectures given by the Old Philosopher, a garrulous, volatile gentleman frequently given to expressing pronounced opinions on any topic of interest to himself. These lectures enjoyed such a popularity with the newspapers' readers that Stephens decided to include most of them in two other works. Three were rewritten for *The Crock of Gold*; twelve others were reworked for the section entitled "There Is a Tavern in the Town," in *Here Are Ladies*.[4] The most interesting aspect of the remaining three may be the reason why they were not published.[5] Two of them (lectures on "The Viceregal Microbe" and on "Government") are both patriotic and comic. In the first the Old Philosopher condemns the English for infecting the Irish with the "microbes" of Plantation, Famine, Trade Restrictions, Sectarianism, and Party Politics. The lecture on Government pairs two villains, policemen and the British government, and makes a plea for internal governance. The third lecture, on lawyers, links the legal profession with those of politics and criminal justice and suggests that those \ who practice these fields are as attractive as rodents, tinned salmon, and other unappetizing objects. These three essays were not reprinted during Stephens' lifetime, probably because he exercised enough critical judgment to realize that their most distinctive qualities are not their artistic merit and unique subject matter but their topicality and their familiar approach to easy Irish targets.

Of Stephens' short stories appearing in Griffith's newspapers during the same time period, seven were rewritten for *Here Are Ladies* and three were worked into *The Crock of Gold*.⁶ "Mrs. Maurice M'Quillan" was not reprinted, probably because it served more as a comic lesson in national pride than a memorable story. Taken as a whole, the short pieces of fiction are the first glimpse at two of Stephens' lifetime interests and pursuits: a desire to analyze the emotional interplay of male-female relationships and a delight in assaulting the bastions of respectability — the law, government, the criminal justice system, and marriage.

At first glance, Stephens' essays published in *Sinn Féin* arrange themselves in two categories: the philosophic and the patriotic. "Poetry," "Tattered Thoughts," "Success," "Imagination," "Good and Evil," "On Politeness," and "Facts," for example, form a set of articles in which he attempts definitions, gives literary advice, creates aphorisms, and works on the development of a theory of aesthetics. Throughout these pieces, the Blakean notion of the Contraries is explored, most particularly in\ "Good and Evil," where those qualities are reviewed in their manifestations as Force and Energy and their distortions in the form of Holiness and Vice. In these works Stephens urges his fellow poets to find their subject matter in the contraries of life: hunger and thirst, love and hate, victory and defeat. For those who are not poets, he urges humanity over civility, personal satisfaction over public acclaim, and honest emotions over polite façades.

In "The Seoinin," Little James takes on Little John Bull, blaming the attempts of the Irish to act, sound, and behave like Englishmen on a system of education in which children study, pray, and recite in English; further, the students read "foolish and weak English novels wherein bad language, bad taste, bad sentiment, and bad morals are plastered together with blood and psuedo bravery." Other patriotic essays, such as "Builders," "The Insurrection of '98," "Patriotism and Parochial Politics," and "Irish Idiosyncrasies" are sometimes humorous, always passionate pleas to learn the Irish language and customs, to remember the heroes of the ancient saga stories, to recognize the more recent leaders of Ireland, and to be more self-critical, enamoured of beauty, ambitious, and future-minded. But the patriotic and the philosophic are not separate approaches; there are Irish references in "Tattered Thoughts," for example, and "Irish Idiosyncrasies" contains a statement on good and evil.

Stephens' book reviews for *Sinn Féin* are memorable only for whimsical asides which have little to do with the subject at hand but a good deal to do with Stephens' high spirits:

> ... whereas in ordinary life filial duty is not only a pious obligation but a matter of personal pride, in literary existence the bar sinister is preferred to the most orderly conjunction.[7]

The reviews do provide clues to Stephens' thoughts on his writing. What he condemns in others — decoration, self-pity, emotional indulgence — he seeks to avoid in his own works. What he praises — distinctive style, craftsmanship, lyricism, energy — are his own best qualities.(1913)

HERE ARE LADIES (1913)

In addition to being a collection of delightful short tales, *Here Are Ladies* is an interesting document because it contains works which are among the first examples of the modern Irish short story. Stephens' characters are clerks and employers, spinster landladies and frustrated housewives, nervous bachelors and smug husbands; the urban counterparts of the priests and peasants found in George Moore's *The Untiled Field*. Their stories are told in a lean, hard style: unnecessary details such as names, specific dates, and places are eliminated; little time is spent on distinguishing characteristics or on dialogue; the narrator gives the reader merely a brief look at a situation. Obvious literary ancestors are Moore, Chekhov, and Galsworthy, but in none of these writers do we find the variety of humor which pervades most of the stories, particularly those written for *Sinn Féin*.

Generally classified as a volume of short fiction, *Here Are Ladies* also contains seven poems and twelve discourses by "the old gentleman." Five of its stories — "A Glass of Beer," "The Triangle," "The Threepenny-Piece," "The Horses," and "The Blind Man" — and the seven poems were late additions to the collection made when Stephens' publisher requested a lengthier manuscript; the book was originally planned to have thirty items — six sets of three stories and the twelve lectures by the "old gentleman."[8] It is not surprising, therefore, that one of the titles suggested by Stephens to his publisher was "Triangles," a figure suggestive of a factor of thirty — three.

Although that title was rejected, given the fact that the additional stories and poems bring the total number of works in the volume to forty-two (still a multiple of three) the title selected has the appropriate number of words. Certainly the number three predominates in the stories. There are groups of three stories, titles suggesting three, situations involving three people, and references to three items. The climax of the stories is often brought about by the presence of three warring parties: a policeman, a young man on the run, and a spinster landlady; a complacent stockbroker, his young wife, and his young clerk; a husband, his wife, and her pretty cousin; a beautiful woman, a poet, and his undistinguished rival; a silly girl, a pompous young suitor, and the rogue she runs away with. An old woman with three teeth can turn into a prophetic hag. An old man can list three good things — a good wife, a good brother, and a good neighbor — and three bad things — to be spied on, to be ruled, and to be asked to give up something you desire to keep.

One of the most delightful of the human triangles is a hilarious version of *Candida* involving a stout matron, a young boy with a highly developed imagination who thinks she is a fairy princess held against her will, and her husband. True to its original source, the young boy goes indignantly into the night after the matron sadly confesses her affection for her giant husband and her determination to remain in her comfortable marriage. Even this melancholy state of affairs is rendered comically by Stephens:

> She told him in a voice that trembled that she would have married him if he had asked her ten years earlier, and urged that she could not fly with him now because, in the first place, she had six children; and, in the second place, it would be against the law; and, in the third place, his mother might object.[9]

Although twelve items were belatedly added to the book, the arrangement of works in this volume is not haphazard.

There are five sections consisting of a poem, a set of three short stories, and a concluding tale. The stories which follow the set of three, usually-comic tales serve as final commentary on the subject matter. The poems also serve a structural purpose: they introduce the topic to be explored, often by presenting a viewpoint in dramatic contrast to that held in the fictional section.

The inclusion of poetry in this volume is an apt decision, because Stephens' poetry written between 1909 and 1918 has a number of thematic links with his fiction. The strong, angry, despairing poems in *Insurrections* have their counterparts in sections of "Hunger" and *The Demi-Gods*. The beauty of nature and the childhood experiences to be found in the *Seumas Beg* poems are reminiscent of scenes in *The Crock of Gold*. The poems in *The Rocky Road* recall the maxims of the philosophers, the teachings of Angus Óg, and the narrator's distrust of the Men of Balor to be found in *The Crock of Gold*; they also link with the tales told by characters in *The Demi-Gods*. The quirks of courtship examined in *Songs from the Clay* are the subject of several stories in *Here Are Ladies*.

A poem, "Women," opens *Here Are Ladies*. In it the poet says: "Listen! If but women were / Half as kind as they are fair / There would be an end to all / Miseries that do appal."[10] These words provide an ironic commentary on "Three Heavy Husbands," the set of stories following the poem in which husbands one and three are tyrants, while husband number two (a bewildered bachelor of many years) does not know how to converse with his new wife. At the end of these stories, the wives have triumphed over their husbands, but it is a deserving victory. The women are battling against men who would try to make them subservient or docile; they defy men who would hold them with words or with marriage vows; and they retaliate by escape, by laughter, and by trickery.

If the poem introduces a touchy subject, the short story following the set, "A Glass of Beer," provides a final dramatic commentary on husbands and wives. In this work the protagonist, who has wished his wife dead, sees himself as her potential murderer:

He had stood unseen with a hammer, a poker, a razor in his hand, on tiptoe to do it. A movement, a rush, one silent rush and it was done! He had revelled in her murder. He had caressed it, rehearsed it, relished it, had jerked her head back, and hacked, and listened to her entreaties bubbling through blood![11]

While it is suggested that he has some cause for these homicidal fantasies — he is living in Paris without friends, money, or the ability to make himself understood when he speaks French — his relationship with his wife, who is dead when the story begins, was always one of violence and hatred. In the story Stephens draws in fine detail a man torn by guilt over the quarrels which preceded his wife's death and further tormented by his neurotic attitude toward the women who walk by the cafe where he sits. The story ends with his recognition of the emptiness and uselessness of his life as an artist, indeed of his entire existence.

The second section, "Three Women Who Wept," opens with a poem, "One and One," which describes an enigmatic woman who faces the narrator-poet, never speaking, stirring the tea she does not drink. The stories which follow this poem, however, do not deal with enigmatic women. The first and third women are quite ordinary people who meet talkative young men who laugh and joke with them and then disappear, leaving the women broken-hearted. The second woman is the mother of a vicious degenerate, who, hated by the world and shunned by the animals he mistreats, is found dead. The only person who weeps over his death is his mother. In the closing story of the section, "Triangle," an equally unenigmatic woman deals in a forthright manner with her husband's infatuation with her cousin by sending the cousin's toy terrier home, unaccompanied, in a basket.

"The Daisies" is a light, graceful poem describing lovers walking hand in hand in a field of flowers. Ironically, it introduces a set of "Three Angry People." The man in the first story claims that his wife has tried to badger him "to a skeleton"; in the following story, a wife who has a fierce temper leads her husband to "understand that there was to be only one head of that household, and that would not be he." In the third story, the female protagonist complains bitterly about men being "surrounded by their wives. They are in gaol and their wives are their warders." Two additional angry people, the seraph Cuchulain and Brien O'Brien, are tossed naked out of heaven by an enraged Rhadamanthus in "The Three-penny-Piece," the short story following this set.

"The Threepenny-Piece" serves as an exemplum of Stephens' technical ability, keen insight into human (and superhuman) nature, and wry humor. This tale of a coin lost by a condemned sinner and found by an inquisitive seraph is told from the point of view of a storyteller who is distinctly Irish; as such the narrator is not above repeating a little malicious gossip and not without respect for the spoken word, even if it consists of a prolonged shout from the depths of Purgatory. Brien O'Brien, the tale's protagonist, steadfastly shouts his refusal to give up the coin, an object originally pressed into his life-less hand on the occasion of his wake. He is so distressed by the loss of his threepenny-piece that he recruits all his fellow sinners into a protest group which threatens to upset the entire organization of Hell. Therein lies the power of the spoken word! Stephens ends his story with a remarkable narra-tive of a voyage through space taken by two spinning creatures, Brien O'Brien and the seraph Cuchulain, as they are propelled earthward by Rhadamanthus, who uses their bodies as an athlete would throw the discus. The description of the journey through space is poetical in its intensity and breathtaking in its speed. For a moment the comedy ceases, but O'Brien and his story end where they began, on earth and ready for another bout of words or fists.

In "Brigid," the poem leading to "Three Young Wives," the poet urges a beautiful young girl not to marry an old man because this man will give her a child and will never leave her and because the poet will suffer "pain and trouble and regret." But the stories which follow suggest other courses of action. A young woman whose beauty has been lost after having smallpox dies in pain during childbirth. A *femme fatale* is described in lurid terms: "a man's head swung at her girdle and she owned the blood that dripped, and her heart tossed rapture and anthem, carol and paean to the air around"; this woman, whose cruelty rebuffs a poet, is later charged by the narrator with killing her husband by her fierce coldness. A third young wife debates leaving her husband because he is boorish, unromantic, and egomaniacal. Conflict between hus-band and wife again breaks open in "The Horses," a story

which portrays the classic picture of a henpecked husband
who is led by his wife's "gently-repressive hand." They have
spent their life together stifled by routine: she tells him when
to come home, what to wear, even what to smoke. Walking
home one night, the husband watches an old horse stoically
standing without moving as its driver proficiently gives it a
whipping. The husband first sympathizes, then identifies with
the horse, fervently wishing that it (he) could be freed and
put out to pasture.[12] He envisions another, Blakean world in
which horses can be embraced by loving children, and so caught
up is he in his dream of horses freely running in the fields
that he jumps onto a train and runs away himself — at least
to the next town, or at least until he runs out of money.

In "Mistress Quiet-Eyes," the poem which precedes "Three
Lovers Who Lost" and "The Blind Man," the narrator views
the fruitfulness of nature: singing birds, colorful flowers, a
woman nursing a child. Its title suggests a source, the Eliza-
bethan lyrics which celebrate the dawning of youthful love.
In the short stories which follow the poem, however, lovers
are judged and found failing. Julia O'Reilly rejects her shy
young suitor for a dashing fellow who will open a shop with
her. The "Princess" — in reality the stout matron with six
children — is rejected by the young boy who has climbed into
her window, because she admits to loving the "ogre" with
whom she lives. Nora MacMahon scorns her father's clerk
when she learns what his occupation is, despite a previous
vow that she could live with "a hut and a crust and the
lover of her heart."

In contrast to these comic tales, "The Blind Man" presents
a protagonist who might have been created by D. H. Lawrence.
The man's tragic flaws are his indifference toward women and
his inability to understand social mores. His mother, who has
disliked him because she has sensed his unwillingness to talk
about the day-to-day "feminine" aspects of life, leaves her
property to his younger brother. In desperation, he marries;
but his wife, her mother, and her two sisters are ugly, unthinking,
ever-talking women. The story ends with a prediction that
his frustration will lead to an act of violence which will end
in his execution.

"Sweet-Apple," the poem following "The Blind Man," is
an abrupt change in mood to a setting of beauty — the fragrance

and shininess of an apple tree in bloom. It is the only poem in *Here Are Ladies* which sets the mood for the stories which follow. These stories of youth, "Three Happy Places," are like the apple on the top of the tree, tempting, free, lovely. In these possibly autobiographical stories, the problems of dealing with a pugnacious bully, the delight of watching a soaring hawk, and the temptation of skipping school are captured in their childish wonder.

No concluding story sets off this section; rather Stephens proceeds with "The Moon," the last poem in the book and an odd choice to introduce "There Is a Tavern in the Town." The poem speaks of a voyage to an ice-covered strand and of death at night; both references look forward to "Desire," a short story in *Etched in Moonlight*, but they have only a peripheral connection to a work in this volume, the tenth discourse in "Tavern" in which the "old gentleman" speaks about the North Pole. The other eleven conversations are on a wide-ranging set of topics: marriage, dancing, smoking, education, drinking, language, poetry, Englishmen, locomotion, shaving, and eating. In the course of these talks, we learn what is to be appreciated — dancing, smoking, drinking, and writing poetry — and to be condemned — formal education, Englishmen, locomotion and exploration (the technological imperative), and marriage. The old man also condemns eating, while partaking of cheese and water biscuits, and talking, while carrying on a lengthy conversation, thus disproving at least two of his own contentions. The discourses may have been based on AE's lectures to his guests at his Sunday evenings, but they have been shaped and enlivened by Stephens. Whether they belong in this volume or not is debatable. They add humor, but they do not fit the thematic aspects of the book or its five-part structure; nor for that matter does "Three Happy Places." *Here Are Ladies* seems to crumble structurally after the five sets of stories, and for that reason some critics who have not noticed its early symmetry find it lacking in design.

Two of the short stories in *Here Are Ladies* found their way into other works. The delightful tale of the threepenny-piece is retold in *The Demi-Gods*. "Three Lovers Who Lost-I" was rewritten as a play, *The Marriage of Julia Elizabeth*, and performed by the Theatre of Ireland group on 17 November 1911 and by a group producing a charity show at the Hardwicke Street Theatre on 26–28 June 1913.

Considered as a unit, the tales based upon early sketches are light and easy of manner. A clerk is described as "a black-haired, slim, frowning young man who could talk like a cascade for ten minutes and be silent for a month." Little else is said about him, but this is enough to prepare the reader for a moment when a fair-haired, romantic young woman leaves her self-assured, possessive, unappreciative husband for the clerk. Another romantic situation is lightly detailed: a young girl falls in love with a man who has a certain insouciance. "He was one of those men who can call ladies by their Christian names. One day he met twenty-four duchesses walking on a red carpet, and he winked at them, and they were all delighted." No physical description of him is provided, but what else do we need to know? Clearly he is a charmer. A brief description of a strong, domineering wife cleaning the house would make an interesting line drawing:

> A long wisp of red hair came looping down on her shoulders. A smear of soot toned down the roses of her cheek, her arms were smothered in soap suds, and the fact that she was wearing a pair of her husband's boots added nothing to her attractions.[13]

The stage is set for the battle between wife and husband, which occurs when he charges across the soapy floor to announce that he has quit his job.

The five stories added by Stephens are his best work technically; their flaw may be that whereas the brief character sketch serves well for humorous stories, more time is needed to develop creatures who display such complex and disturbing qualities as misogyny and sexual repression. What is sketched here is dark in tone, ugly in nature: women's lips are "thin red gashes" that suggest "rat-traps," or their clothing is dirty and they wear irritating, flapping slippers, or they hammer away at men in conversation.

In July 1913, Stephens wrote Howe that he felt there were "real good things in Here are Ladies, but it is unequal[.] I will be very anxious for your opinion on half a dozen of its contents."[14] The copy of the book which he inscribed for

Howe has pencil marks beside three entries. "A Glass of Beer,"
"The Triangle," and "The Blind Man" — and numbers beside
three sets of stories: "2" before "Three Women Who Wept";
"1" before "Three Angry People," and "2" before "Three
Young Wives."[15] If these are the six stories Stephens singled
out for praise, they make an interesting grouping around a
theme which deserves further exploration, sexual politics.

Looking at Stephens' writings throughout his life the reader
finds a number of works devoted to the unhappy aspects of
male-female relationships. According to Stephens' male characters, women are highly critical, they demand that their husbands pay attention to them even after marriage, they have
their own interests and talk a good deal about matters which
are not important to men, and they seek control. It is this
last-named quality which leads to an inevitable clash, and
indeed, in many of Stephens' stories there is a verbal, psychological, even physical, battle.[16] This view of man and woman as
polar opposites in constant conflict has its beginnings in two
of Stephens' favorite sources, Theosophical doctrine, in which
there is reference to opposing forces such as good and evil,
and Blake, with his insistence on the warring Contraries. The
conflict between man and woman may be treated comically
or sentimentally or in both fashions in the same novel. Compare,
for example, the flirtation of Mary and her policeman with
the potentially serious relationship between the young lodger
and Mary, still unrealized at the close of *The Charwoman's
Daughter*, or compare the battles of the Thin Woman and the
Philosopher with the union of Caitilin and Óg.

Although his early works explore marital strife extensively,
Stephens never stopped interpolating his views on the subject
into his fiction. One of his first short stories, "Mrs. Jerry Gorman," contains a lecture on how wives should treat their husbands. *Here Are Ladies* explores a variety of marital conflicts,
while several tales in *Etched in Moonlight* are concerned with
unhappy marriages. A remark in his last novel is an echo
of a complaint added to his first:

Now it is a curious thing that women awaken in the morning
uncomely but gay, while men arise to the new day as though
they were being reborn into unhappiness; for at dawn man
is ill-tempered, and a great discoverer of insult.[17]

. . . in the morning husbands are unwieldy, morose creatures
without joy, without lightness, lacking even the common,
elemental interest in their own children, and capable of detest-
ably misinterpreting the conversation of their wives.[18]

In one early short story, "Mrs. Maurice M'Quillan," an
easy-going Irishman who is wedded to a woman with pretensions
of gentility must order her pro-British brother out of the house
before he can gain back control of his marriage. A more violent,
unpublished story, "Mrs. Timothy Murphy," describes in detail
the means by which a woman bests her drunken spouse. After
a particularly fierce battle in which he has given her a severe
beating, he falls asleep in bed, and she sews him into the
sheets. Then she calmly beats him with a cane until she is
tired; gives him a glass of water and beats him again; gives
him breakfast, beats him; gives him dinner, beats him; goes
to sleep, beats him on wakening; and so on for two days.
On the third day of this battle, she cuts him loose from the
sheets, warning him that if he gets drunk again, she will take
the same action.

The murder instinct is aroused in the battles between men
and women in "A Glass of Beer," "The Blind Man," "Three
Young Wives — II," and other stories in *Here Are Ladies*. It
is also found in the quarrels between Eileen ni Cooley and
Patsy Mac Cann in *The Demi-Gods*, and between Maeve and
Conachúr in *Deirdre*. Stephens' women are always resourceful,
independent, strong. They are also impulsive and irrational.
What prevents eternal warfare is their more positive qualities:
their intuition, their pity for male weakness, and their maternal
instinct. These saving graces seem noticeably absent in most
of the short stories in *Etched in Moonlight*.

ETCHED IN MOONLIGHT (1928)

Of the short stories published in *Here Are Ladies*, "A Glass
of Beer," "The Horses," and "The Blind Man" link most
closely with the works of Stephens included in *Etched in Moonlight*. The emotions which were barely kept in control in
the first book are now on a rampage; avarice, envy, despair,
shame, jealousy, malice, guilt, anger consume the characters.

Husband and wife clash or endure a grinding poverty with no release short of death.

Written in 1918 during a period in which Stephens was profoundly depressed by World War I, there are no happy endings in these stories. The mood ranges from irritability to desperation. Stephens' whimsy is gone; his humor is sardonic; there is no light touch to relieve the tension. The characters find no comfort in their settings. A husband seeks a different life and finds only death; a woman and her children cannot escape the horror of starvation; a man cannot avoid meeting a reminder of his past; another is forced by his obsessive thoughts to relive the past; in several works the indifference, the inhumanity of man toward his fellowman brings down the helpless victim. In the streets, in offices, in homes, in the countryside, there is no escape.

In a letter to Lady Leconfield dated 31 March 1928, Stephens defended parts of the work. "I think most people are disappointed in my new book. Short stories are (somehow) unsatisfactory. But I'll swear that three of them were worth writing."[19] Stephens does not identify his choices, but they can be surmised: "Hunger," "Etched in Moonlight," and "Desire" are worthy of further commentary.[20]

"Hunger," a story which was originally published in 1918 under the pseudonym of James Esse, is a relentless portrait of misery comparable to that presented in the nineteenth century by William Carleton in *The Black Prophet: A Tale of the Famine*. Like Carleton, Stephens is representing the psychological and physical effects of hunger on the poor. Stephens' characters, like Carleton's peasants, face starvation with optimism, then anxiety, and finally with stunned, silent misery. Stephens has written of poverty before in *The Charwoman's Daughter*, but Mary pawning her mother's goods and Mrs. Cafferty worrying about her children are not people broken by hunger. This story of a family living in a Dublin tenement begins with a crippled child, a husband desperate for work, and five hungry people and moves forward unrelentingly to outbreaks of illness, futile attempts at begging, the indignities of total poverty, and the final inevitable ending, death, in this case of two children and the husband. The tale is all the more memorable because this agonizing account of impending starvation and death is conveyed with a clarity and straightforwardness as objective and as crushing as a social worker's report:

> The distinguishing mark of her family had been thinness, it was now bonyness.[21]

> Her earnings were small, for she could not get in touch with people. That too is a trade and must be learned. They recognised her at a distance as a beggar, and she could only whisper to the back of a head or a cold shoulder.[22]

> . . . the gentleman called on the following day to investigate, and was introduced to a room swept almost as clean of furniture as a dog kennel is; to the staring, wise-eyed child who lived in a chair; and to the quiet morsel of death that lay in a cot by the wall.[23]

The tone here is restrained, too restrained. Stephens seems to have set his teeth to keep from screaming with rage and pain. He later said that the story was true and that he wrote it down to get it out of his mind. If so, he permanently fixed it in the minds of his readers.

Another time and another setting are presented in "Etched in Moonlight," but this short story also deals with insanity, cruelty, and death. The tale reveals the influence of Dunsany, but it lacks that energy which Stephens sought to emulate. Stephens worried over the story, as he explained to Walter H. Parker:

> The title story may seem dull: the excuse is, that I wanted to do a certain kind of thing in a certain kind of way, & perhaps that thing can not be done in that way: to dispense with action, or to transfer action into the mind itself is not an easy thing.[24]

Superficially, the tale is that of a triangle: two men love a beautiful woman. The consuming jealousy felt by the man who is rejected moves him from disdain for their concerned looks to disgust for their gestures of affection. His revenge is to leave them trapped in a building from which he believes they cannot escape and to flee the country. His inability to forget this deed brings him back to the land twelve years

The Art and Craft of Prose 135

later; here he finds that his friends have not died, and here
he encounters fear, terror, and finally madness. This story is
a dream told by a narrator who has a different physique and
personality, who lives in a different time in history than the
character in his dream, and who does not account for why
he should have such a nightmare. Perhaps the most unsatisfactory aspect of the story is that this narrator is so briefly introduced that his relationship to the man he becomes in his dream
cannot be, or is not, explained.

"Desire" returns to the everyday Dublin world of "Hunger,"
but its central image is that of a prophetic dream, not unlike
the one in "Etched in Moonlight." Here again is a nightmare
from which a character pays a terrible price to escape. The
story begins with the metamorphosis of a totally, almost boringly,
predictable man into an excited recipient of a gift commonly
given in fairy and folk tales: one wish which will come true.
What is significant about the discussion which follows between
the man and his wife, however, is less his choice than their
disagreement over what he should choose. He rejects wealth,
although she clearly would have chosen it. He also spurns
wisdom, because it would isolate him from his peers, not because
it would make her uncomfortable. His choice, to remain at
his present age until he dies, distresses her because she faces
the prospect of aging while he retains his vigor; he doesn't
seem to recognize how threatening his choice is to her, or
how selfish he seems to her.

The climax of the story, the wife's dream of a sea voyage
toward snow and ice, is a vision recalling the ending of Joyce's
"The Dead"; it is death toward which the woman is going.
The dream also reflects the woman's concern with material
goods (she is greatly concerned with her baggage and frequently
inspects her belongings), her lack of warmth toward her husband, and her dependence upon social mores. Like "Etched
in Moonlight" terror is ahead; at the close of the story she
wakes to find herself touching the cold, rigid, dead body of
her husband. His wish has been fulfilled in a terrifyingly exact
manner.

"Desire" is a story with links to other tales on the subject
of unhappy marriages. The old quarrel between the Philosopher
representing Male Reason and the Thin Woman who is Female
Emotion is reworked here. The contrasting responses of the

characters to the husband's wish to stay the same age is indicative of this split: he has a rational explanation for his wish; she, an emotional response. The two characters in this work must bear full responsibility for what happens to them: the husband for making his wish without considering his wife's feelings; the wife for not understanding her husband's wish as a desperate attempt to stop the ravages of time and to escape the nets of marriage. Three short stories not included in *Etched in Moonlight* deal with similar subjects. "Crepe de Chine" and "The Birthday Party" chronicle the story of failed marriages, straying husbands, shrewish wives; "Sawdust" describes a poor widow who sits alone in a snug, drinking until her memories drive her to madness and suicide.

The four additional stories in the volume deal with other "domestic goblins." In "Schoolfellows" a man finds himself saddled with an old acquaintance down on his luck and learns to do what his schoolmate's family has done, reject him, but not without guilt and anger taking their toll on him. "Darling" is an ironic title, referring to a manner of address used in the first stages of a marriage which falls apart when the man loses his job, his wife, and his home due to the cruel pranks played upon him by his fellow employees. Another, more disagreeable marriage is described in "The Wolf," in which the only solace for an ungainly, unloved husband is drink. "The Boss" views the world of employment from an unusual angle for Stephens; it is a sympathetic look at an employer who finds out how intolerable the hierarchal structure can be when he must "sack" a forthright employee. In all of these works the verities are missing: friendship based on old school ties frays; marriages disintegrate; the comradeship of fellow workers is lacking; it isn't worthwhile to succeed in business. There is a failure to communicate: comradeship and love are gone. Even little children (usually portrayed by Stephens as sensitive, outgoing creatures) run from the clumsy, drunken country bumpkin in "The Wolf" who only seeks their attention.

The stories in *Etched in Moonlight* provide evidence of Stephens' efforts to polish his short fiction: these are precisely cut, well-mounted gems. Their flaw may be a point of view put forward by Stephens in the Preface to *The Sword in the Soul* by Roger Chauviré. In his introduction Stephens maintains that narration of action is more important than characterization in fiction.

For there are many multitudes of people in the world, but there are very few actions: and, not alone by its mere rarity but also because of its greater intensity, action must be considered as paramount to the actors, and these latter must be, as it were, unfairly treated if the pace and emotion of the fundamental action are to be thoroughly arrived at.[25]

The characters in Stephens' short stories are often anonymous; it is their deeds, their internal conflicts, or the events crushing them which the reader remembers. When this method works, in "Hunger" for example, where the anonymity is a counterpoint to a tale of immense human suffering, it produces a memorable short story. Too often, however, the story cannot survive such impersonal treatment and is quickly forgotten.

MISCELLANEOUS PROSE WRITINGS

Arthur Griffith: Journalist and Statesman (1922) consists of two articles; one praising Griffith's courage, endurance, charity, devotion to the Irish poets of the nineteenth century, and his ability as an editor and politician; the other recalling Stephens' shock over the news of Griffith's death. The work emphasizes the importance of Griffith in Stephens' life and makes even more understandable his determination to undertake his version of the *Táin*.

How St. Patrick Saves the Irish (1931) is a published version of a story told by Stephens in March 1928 in *Radio Times* and the *New York Times*. It is the charming tale of a decision made by St. Patrick and St. Brigid that Patrick ask Christ's permission to sit in judgment in heaven of Irishmen, thus allowing the Irish to avoid the "immovable, unescapable, terrific" Rhadamanthus. In the story, the Irish people are assured of two advocates; when St. Patrick receives approval of their plan, he and Brigid discuss the outcome:

"You will be very careful," she said to St. Patrick.
"Surely, I will," the great saint answered.
"But if," said St. Brigid, and the very heart within her was shocked, "but if a bad Irishman is brought before you —"
"I'll convert him," said St. Patrick.[26]

"A Rhinoceros, Some Ladies, and a Horse," Stephens' last work, is usually classified as a short story, although its author claimed it was to be a chapter in an autobiography. Whatever the case, it is as fresh, irreverent, and engaging as the tale of Saints Brigid and Patrick. Stephens returns in this work to a favorite subject, and gives a picture of adolescence unsurpassed in its lunacy:

> One day, in my first job, a lady fell in love with me. It was quite unreasonable, of course, for I wasn't wonderful: I was small and thin, and I weighed much the same as a largish duck-egg. I didn't fall in love with her, or anything like that. I got under the table, and stayed there until she had to go wherever she had to go to.[27]

The wonder is not that two animals and two women fall in love with the youthful Stephens in this story; it is that only four creatures are mentioned. Surely everyone loves such exuberance.

BBC BROADCASTS

Stephens' first talk on the BBC, "I Remember: Reminiscences of J. M. Synge," launched a career that lasted twenty-two years. Like his other forms of artistic endeavor, radio broadcasting came after years of preparation; in this case his lecture tours of the United States and his poetry readings on both sides of the Atlantic served him in good stead. Further, his narrative style from first to last was that of a storyteller in whom speech and prose were not separate entities. As Lloyd Frankenberg points out, Stephens' "writing sounds like talk, and so does his talk."[28] As the years passed the topics changed but the speaker remained the same: sprightly in approach, jocular in tone, confident in attitude.

Frequently he began with a short, provocative remark:

> Future criticism will have plenty to say about Yeats, for he was odd as a man, odd as a poet, and odd as a dramatist.[29]

> Great men do go out of date pretty fast.[30]

Joyce was strangely in love with his own birthday and with mine.[31]

One day, away in a place, I saw a spider.[32]

Of course I have to pretend that I know how I came to write my poems, but I'll also have to admit, as between us, that I only know in a sort of a way.[33]

From these markers, Stephens and his listeners start on adventures which lead everywhere. There are stories of odd incidents about even odder people and animals. There is Mannin who seems to be a descendant of Fionn, when he describes how he lifted his pet cow under the crook of his left hand and climbed fifty feet up a cliff. There is Mildred, a delightfully talkative, very fat, highly emotional lady who falls in love with a goat which will only eat its fodder out of her lap. And Nicodemus, a bull who runs after people because he wants to sit in their laps.

Many talks are devoted to friends who are writers and to those works which he likes: Yeats and "Byzantium," AE and "Reconciliation," Joyce, *Ulysses*, and *Finnegans Wake*. The object of the talk is rarely to provide scholarly insight; instead it is to convey impressions of the artist and his work. The listener remembers the incidents which encapsulate character: Griffith in Africa, deathly ill but so defiant that he plays handball for seven hours straight in order to break his fever; AE solemnly explaining that he gave up meditation because he found himself turning into a pillar of fire twenty feet high and feared that in one more second he would become a cinder which would have to be carried away with tongs; Yeats reciting Donne's poetry to his three-year-old son and receiving as reply a roar, "Go away, Man!" The broadcasts also record interests and preoccupations found throughout Stephens' works. They hold droll examinations of garrulous country people, maternal spiders, athletic young men, and hungry cows. They contain fond recollections of friends and acquaintances and equally intimate introductions to favorite writers Stephens did not know. Consider for example, this remarkable survey of English literature:

Nearly all Chaucer's poems are about people — they are the nicest people in poetry, as Chaucer is the nicest poet in poetry. Spenser sings a lot about "lady gents," which is his odd way of putting it, and these ladies are among the best gents in English. The best gent in English is, of course, Milton's Devil. Herrick's poems are rarely about love — they are all about making love, and they are lovely. Too many of Wordsworth's soliloquies are about "human nature's daily food" — he tends to conceive that a piece of meat and two veg. is a kind of woman, and who are we to disagree with him![34]

THE SHORT STORIES IN PERSPECTIVE

Given his audience and his publisher, it is not surprising that the items Stephens submitted to Griffith's newspapers had some political import, whether they were essays particularly nationalistic in bent or short stories. The three tales published in *Sinn Féin* which were then rewritten for *The Crock of Gold* still contain an attack on the establishment, in this case those Irish employers and country people who ape the British in their concern for productivity and gentility at the expense of more humane concerns. In another fictional sketch, "Mrs. Maurice M'Quillan," Stephens again attacks those Irish, here Mrs. M'Quillan and Percy Farrell, whom he condemns as "*seoinins*."

When he included eight of his short stories written for *Sinn Féin* in *Here Are Ladies*, he modified them, eliminating names and other details, making the tales less Irish, more "continental" in approach. Written in Paris, the last five additions to *Here are Ladies* are particularly lacking in the nationalistic tone found in his earlier writing. "A Glass of Beer," for example, could be about an expatriate American, "The Blind Man" could be the story of an English farmer, "The Triangle" and "The Horses" are domestic dramas with no ethnic aspect to them; only "The Threepenny-Piece" is Irish in flavor and thus can be transplanted into *The Demi-Gods* as one of the stories told on the country roads of Ireland.

Again in *Etched in Moonlight*, with the notable exception of "Hunger," a short story which was originally published in 1918 as a separate volume under the pseudonym of James

Esse, the stories are precise, careful observations of nameless characters who might live in any big city. What makes the stories Irish — and thus links them to the Irish writers of today — is their "hammered," "polished" prose. Stephens' perfection of his craft, a traditional concern of the Irish storytellers and poets, can be observed in all his writing. Coming after *The Charwoman's Daughter* and *The Crock of Gold*, the short stories combine realism (precise description, a lean structure, a realistic setting, apt words) and fantasy (a castle and a dungeon, a wish come true, a world of demons, ogres, and madmen). In one volume, *Etched in Moonlight*, the extremes meet in "Hunger" and the title story, in "Darling" and "Desire."

When he was not spinning fables about his friends in his BBC broadcasts, Stephens spun a few about himself. Those that are avowedly autobiographical compound fact and fiction: references to his small size and recollections of the gestures of love proffered by a rhinoceros; a poignant description of a dying dog coupled with an insistence that the dog hunted for and shared food with him for two months; a sprightly discussion of fish in general and the narration of a supposed underwater conversation with one which is twenty-five feet in length. Although his broadcasts were not transcriptions of short stories, they certainly contained stories, with the same economy of technique, freshness of approach, vivid descriptive power, and impish good humor that the reader finds in his best works of short fiction.

6 The Marriage of the Contraries

Frank O'Connor called Stephens the Irish writer with "the most agile mind. . . . a sort of literary acrobat, doing hair-raising swoops up in the roof of the tent."[1] Stephens certainly needed agility and bravado to move as he did from one genre to another, producing novels, poems, short stories, essays, book reviews, radio scripts, and journalistic accounts. His best piece of journalism, *The Insurrection in Dublin*, is a powerful summation of events, impressions, and rumors gathered on the site of the Easter Uprising by a sympathetic but not strident observer. The final appeals he makes in that account, to England for a fair settlement and to Ireland for a renewed commitment, are so clear-headed, forceful, and highly effective that it is hard to imagine him taking another approach to the subject. And yet he does, in *Green Branches* where the same events produce a set of poems both sensitive to the tradition of the elegy and moving beyond that tradition to a personal affirmation of national pride.

When Stephens works within one medium, the results may also be infinitely varied. He fills *Insurrections*, his first volume, with poems displaying the heights of emotion, but far from being singular in direction, the moods swing from anger to pity, from independence to need, from fear to calm. Early pieces of prose, specifically those works written for *Sinn Féin*, are rebellious pieces advocating Irish defiance on the grounds of the suppressive political, economic, and legal measures taken by the English; but other pieces published in the same newspaper during the same period take a comic rather than an indignant approach to these incendiary topics. Often within the same piece he presents two points of view. In *The Demi-Gods* he finds life on the country roads both a romantic adventure and a frantic search for food and shelter. Country people are affectionately portrayed, but they are not without cruelty and viciousness.

His poems throughout his early and middle periods cover a multitude of subjects: murder, patriotism, childhood, senility, madness, the calm beauty of nature. Short stories from the same periods investigate the lives of prosaic husbands, sadistic youths, pathetic housewives, shrews, rejected lovers, exuberant schoolboys. In his first novels he introduces charladies, tinkers, gods, angels, shepherdesses, and others; combines fairy and realistic settings; and mixes psychological analysis, philosophical debate, comic banter, and romance. He moves from settings in the slums and comfortable homes of Dublin to country estates, camps on the roadside, cottages in the forest, mountain caves, and county fairs. In his later poetry where technical experimentation is limited, the subject matter abstract, and the tone familiar, there are still the disparate sources: Eastern religion and thought, contemporary Irish politics, Romantic Period poetry, among other areas.

Nowhere is his infinite variety displayed more fully than in his adaptations of Gaelic material. He makes selections which allow him to present legends dealing with betrayal, love, battle, political intrigue, murder, magical transformation, heroic exploits, marriage, and adultery. His cast of legendary characters includes the extraordinarily beautiful and the exceptionally ugly, youthful adventurers and ancient sages, maidens in distress and fierce female warriors, quarrelsome swineherds and courteous heroes. If only one aspect of his work in adapting these legends is examined, his comic genius, there are many traditional forms of humor to cite: whimsy, irony, fantasy, satire, parody, the portrayal of the grotesque, word play.

Stephens may have been an amateur athlete, but he was a professional craftsman. For him, invention meant refinement as well as conception. The manuscripts of his works reveal his role as a self-critic. Additions which he made to the drafts bring color or sharpness, the unusual or the specific, the melodious or the humorous; deletions eliminated the easy or the predictable, the superfluous or the overworked. Throughout the manuscripts he paid equal attention to the different elements of his art: the wry remark, the philosophical speculation, the curses and the pleas, the lyrical description, and the earthy dialogue. His writing, whatever the genre, was painstakingly reworked, but with the revisions came the rewards, the achievement of a distinctive style and recognition as an artist.

Stephens may have complained at times about an inability to concentrate on his writing or a difficulty in producing the effects which he sought, but he did not suffer from lack of topics. A number of projects were begun but not finished during his lifetime. These included at least six plays, a novel, a project entitled "La Comedie Humaine of Ireland," many poems, and several sketches intended for an autobiography. Despite the lack of these additional proofs of literary talent, and despite what Hilary Pyle classifies as a "small" output, there is sufficient work to judge his ability.[2]

As AE prophesied in 1910 and again in 1912, Stephens' poetry has been eclipsed by his prose.[3] It is not surprising to find, fifty years after AE's remarks, Gerald Dewitt Sanders and M. L. Rosenthal's contention, in a commentary on modern poets, that "James Stephens, despite his fine ear for Irish folk-speech and his charm and immediacy and imagination, seems to have receded with that Celtic revival of which he was so much a part."[4] Much of the poetry is dated, heavy-handed, repetitive, too dependent. Stephens himself recognized these qualities when he judged a number of poems as unworthy of reprinting in *Collected Poems*. The list of rejected poems is too lengthy to be included here, but among those which he particularly disliked and labeled as derivative, too personal, facile, or gauche are "The Seeker," "The Winged Tramp," "The Earth Gods," "The Crown of Thorns," "The Red-Haired Man," "Woman Shapes," and "The Liar." His judgment on these works is hardly disputable.

Despite these creative failures, there are other poems which meet his standards of delicacy of movement, "neatness," and "sparkle" and which also have received favorable critical commentary: "What Tomas an Buile Said in a Pub," "The Red-Haired Man's Wife," "To the Four Courts, Please," "The Snare," "The Goat Paths," "Deirdre," "The Coolun," "Skim-

Milk," and "Righteous Anger," for instance. As Randall Jarrell points out, Stephens' poems have their faults, "but they have in them so much warmth and pain and humor, so many of the concerns of human beings like ourselves, that it is natural for us to be attracted to them."[5]

If the poetry sometimes falls flat, it is equally true that there are awkward sections in the prose, particularly where Stephens has interpolated his own theories into the text. In Chapter XXI of *The Charwoman's Daughter*, his discussion of the complex relationship between men and women is an interruption of Mary and Mrs. Cafferty's conversation, and his lecture on Thought, Justice and reason in Chapter XIII of *The Crock of Gold* brings the plot to a complete standstill. His appearances in the enthusiastic first person are not always welcome. Chapter XXXII of *The Demi-Gods* is devoted to a coy conversation between Stephens and a donkey. It begins, "'Little ass, quoth I, 'how is everything with you?'" This conjunction of character and creator shows how charming sweetness can occasionally become annoying saccharine.

His method of only briefly sketching a character sometimes works in the short stories, but is more often successful in the novels. Caitilin Ni Murrachu is never described, but what we learn about her is more important than details of her face and body. We discover that she loves children and animals, that she is lonely without adult companionship, that she is capable of understanding concepts, and that she is in need of fulfillment. Her two lovers are described only in the most casual manner, in order to contrast hair coloring and facial expression. In the novel these three characters are developed in terms of their words, actions, and thoughts so that Caitilin's decision between Angus Óg and Pan is understandable, even instructive. There is no time for that careful development in the short stories, and many of them court dismissal because their characters lack definition and vitality and thus are never real enough for the reader to care about them.

These lapses in craft are infrequent and not typical of Stephens' work as a whole. His positive aspects have been enumerated throughout this book: an unerring selection of the right image, an accurate reproduction of speech patterns, a sense of timing, an exact turn of a phrase, a quickness of thought, a lack of affectation, and a comic and sympathetic nature. As far as he was concerned, rather than being crowned king of the leprecauns, he would prefer to be known by Gogarty's title, "the last of the shanachies."[6]

The shanachies, those Irish story-tellers who blended supernatural acts and realistic details into stories, were sought-after figures in ancient Ireland, for they were not only the oral transmitters of legend but also entertainers and teachers, adding details to please or instruct their listeners. This reverence for the story-teller is reflected in four works by Stephens, "The Story of Tuan Mac Cairill," "Mongan's Frenzy," *In the Land of Youth*, and *The Demi-Gods*. In the two stories included in *Irish Fairy Tales*, Finnian, the abbot of Moville, is so moved by Tuan's narration that he interjects, "continue, my love," "tell on, my love," and other encouragements, and he invites the story-tellers of Ireland to his monastery in order to write down their tales so that they may be preserved. The story-teller's ability to improve upon his tale is also illustrated in "Mongan's Frenzy." When Finnian hears the tale from Cairidè, he objects to a comic portion in which a cleric is mistreated. Cairidè agrees that the incident is "ill done," but he secretly resolves to keep the incident and to add to it the abbot's objections when next he recites the story.

When Nera tells his adventures to Queen Maeve's court, his listeners forget to drink their ale, mead, and wine, so filled are they with "astonishment" and "reverie." Maeve also astounds her audience. Her narration, like that of Cairidè, suggests that the ancient story-tellers added details as they progressed: she inserts contemporary references, explanations of motives, advertisements for her warriors, and even hints of her marital infidelities into her story of Etain.

The Demi-Gods has more modern story-tellers, Finaun, Billy the Music, Caeltia, and Art; and even though their stories are drawn from other than Gaelic sources, the response of their audience is that afforded to the traditional story-teller. Both Eileen Ni Cooley and Mary Mac Cann claim that they could listen to a story "for a day and a night." When Patsy speaks approvingly of Caeltia and Billy's stories, Billy tells him about an old man who was one of the best of the shanachies:

> "He was a gifted man, for he would tell you a story about nothing at all, and you'd listen to him with your mouth

open and you afraid that he would come to the end of it soon, and maybe it would be nothing more than the tale of how a white hen laid a brown egg. He would tell you a thing you knew all your life, and you would think it was a new thing. There was no old age in that man's mind, and that's the secret of story-telling."[7]

It is clear from these passages that Stephens is aware of the story-teller's prerogative to change and expand a story by developing or justifying the action, "improving" the dialogue, adding descriptive material, and inserting explanatory remarks. In Stephens' contribution to the Irish Literary Revival, that is, those books based on Gaelic materials, as well as in the earlier novels and short fiction, we often observe the ancient story-teller's rapport with his audience, his practice of creating new material, and his enjoyment of his profession.

Stephens' work, like that of Yeats, extends well into the twentieth century, and in *Deirdre* and other works, he not only illustrates the traditions of the shanachies but also the interest of the writers of the Literary Revival in the presentation of legends and folk lore. He was a part of that constantly shifting, frequently quarreling group, and like Yeats, Lady Gregory, AE, Moore, and the others, he wrote in English but adapted, made reference to, or worked within Irish legend, folklore, or folklife. He described local scenes, although his were not restricted to rural settings, and he placed clarity, technical experimentation, and literary craftsmanship above nationalistic sentiment. Like other writers in Dublin in the 1900s, he experienced and reacted to the conflicting desires to live in Ireland and to be an exile; he responded negatively to Irish parochialism, materialism, and Anglophilia; and he espoused better living conditions for the poor. Like AE and Yeats he expressed an interest in the mystical as manifested in Theosophical thought, Indian philosophy and religion, spiritualism, and the occult.

Because he managed to escape "the nets" of religion and country, the views expressed on these subjects in the works are steadfastly unorthodox and sometimes mocking. He could utilize aspects of Theosophical thought in *The Demi-Gods*, but he could also joke in that work about matters of the occult. He could argue for Ireland's independence with enough passion to satisfy Arthur Griffith, but he could also reject the narrow views of the Sinn Féiners and the Gaelic Leaguers by taking a less political, more reasoned approach toward national independence.

Stephens' work also serves as a model for the modern Irish writers. In his work he presents two themes which have their bases in the historical and socio-economic aspects of modern Ireland, *dispossession* (the blight upon the land) and *disaffection*, (the curse upon its people). Stephens and the Irish writers who follow after him provide us with settings which include city as well as country scenes, but in which the land, lost or untilled, is always a dynamic presence. In these works the story is centered in the family unit — strained marriages, quarrels between parents and children, uneasy relationships among neighbors, but also happy childhood memories and recalled moments of tenderness and love.

Stephens' works reveal a personality like that of Ireland: brooding, highly comic, and bold. His novels and poems show us the gaiety and the loneliness of the Irish people: their estrangement from the land which was once theirs and their desire to return to an earlier, pastoral period; their animosities and suspicions; their flights of fantasy; and their love of words. His works are filled with the sunshine and thunder, lush vegetation and dirty slums, green trees and bloody combats of Ireland.

Although he had an ability to marry the opposites, including those of time and space, in one area he set up no contrasts. His best writing concentrates solely on Ireland. *Insurrections* and *The Charwoman's Daughter* provide affectionate or grimly accurate pictures of Dublin; *The Crock of Gold* and *The Demi-Gods* expand the setting to include the Irish countryside; *Deirdre*, *Irish Fairy Tales*, *Reincarnations*, and *In the Land of Youth* expand the time frame to include vivid, bold recreations of Ireland's past. Whatever the subject, it is an Irishman who is telling the story.

Richard J. Loftus has pointed out that Stephens' mature work is informed by his vision of "a nation of love and kindness and joy."[8] His love of Ireland is immediately apparent in his writing. Since Stephens once said, possibly to console his later biographers, that every book is a catalog of the author's own "likes, dislikes, hopes, fears, aspirations and mentality," what other aspects of his life are mirrored in his works?[9]

Details of his childhood are not known, but it was hardly the happy period of innocence lived by Seumas and Brigid in *The Crock of Gold*. The Seumas Beg poems come closer to mark, for they are not just whimsical, endearing looks at the age of innocence, but careful studies of the uglier aspects of growing up, the complicating emotions of fascination and revulsion felt when encountering a terrifying adult, for example. In James Joyce's short story, "An Encounter," a young boy meets an enigmatic stranger whose green eyes first suggest mysterious adventure but whose behavior is frightening and repellent. Seumas Beg also meets a series of bewildering characters: a crazed woman screaming for a lost child, a man beating a young girl, a pirate, an angel, a devil, a giant, a man on a flying carpet, a mad man carrying a knife. The most fearful of these people is a man dressed in green, whose attempt to lure the young boy away when his mother is gone with promises of a castle and money, has the same uneasy aspects of Joyce's "Encounter." It is probably revealing that Seumas Beg is a story-teller himself and that he is a fatherless child.

Certain other, recurrent artistic subjects mirror aspects of Stephens' life, namely, his realistic depiction of the Dublin slums and his sympathy for the poor, his understanding of the tedium, the dreary existence of the clerks who populate Dublin's offices, his keen analysis of the tensions of a single-parent family, and his romanticized view of the healing aspect of the wild countryside. Even his assumption of the return of the ancient gods, in *The Crock of Gold* and elsewhere, coupled as it is with a certain gleeful irreverence, is too deeply felt not to be a part of the author.

Structural considerations may also reflect personal characteristics. Was his need to establish roots the reason behind the structure of his first three novels? In these works the characters move in a circle which always brings them back home. Mary Makebelieve briefly envies the comfortable world of the middle-class, but when she finds herself in it, she rushes back to her dwelling in the slums. Various expeditions set off for all points in *The Crock of Gold*, but the explorers all end where they began, in the forest of the enchanted mountain. The travelers on the country roads in *The Demi-Gods* end where they began, the burial site of the angels' belongings. Stephens himself tried to touch home base as often as he could, by trips back to

Ireland, exchanges of letters, and frequent personal contact with visiting friends.[10]

The contradictions found in his works also reflect his life. Charity and injustice, liberty and exploitation, glee and indignation were the elements which filled Stephens' mind and paper. The terrors recorded in his writings were those which he knew personally — dark nights, hunger, illness, the tortuous gropings of the mind, old age. The joys were familiar, too — childhood games, the love of a man and a woman, the sights and sounds of nature, the pleasures of friendship, dancing, and conversation. Stephens' characters were the people he met or believed to exist: tinkers, gods, philosophers, angels, servants, queens. The tone of his works, like that of his conversations with friends, shifted from satirical to merry, gentle to malicious, relaxed to furious. Whatever the topic or occasion, Stephens' approach was the same: to sing, not to weep.[11] And the lessons to be learned in his writings were those he set for himself: to conquer fear, guilt, the pressures of time and space; to discover oneself, to give of oneself, and to seek inner peace.

Although he does not provide a complete catalog of his characters' physical qualities, even in those works based on Irish saga materials where some of these data are available, he does stress an aspect of characterization which suggests a personal interest. He closely examines the emotional states of his characters, finding particularly fascinating those people who are obsessed or deeply committed. The contemporary narrator of "Etched in Moonlight" bears resemblance to two otherwise totally dissimilar characters, the Policeman in *The Charwoman's Daughter* and King Conachúr in *Deirdre*, because all three exhibit a sexual possessiveness which will lead to a violent ending of a romantic relationship.

Stephens' delight in "being" himself into another creature, in transporting himself into the consciousness of an animal and recording that animal's thought, reaches new heights when he progresses from the purely comic conversations in the early novels between two children and a cow, an angel and a spider, and the author and a donkey, to the later recording of the complex sensations of human beings who change into the shape of an animal, namely, Tuan's thoughts as he moves through several reincarnations, Etain's sense of the lightness, the freedom of being a flying creature, and Saeve and Tuiren's transfigu-

rations in the forms of a deer and a dog. Even when dealing
with shifting time schemes and settings, he brings to the notion
of another time, another place an acute sense of the effect
such changes have on the personality of ordinary human beings,
such as Nera and Brótiarna and on those more remarkable
creatures, Becfola, Becuma, Mongan, Art, Maeve, and Fionn.
His adaptation of the legends about Etain, in particular, traces
her life over "more than a thousand years" in terms of her
responses to various lands, time schemes, and bodily forms.

Stephens' keen analysis of human emotions, sharpened during
the years of his prose writing, reaches its peak in the last
two novels. The torment of jealous possessiveness, only sketched
in the Policeman's reactions toward Mary Makebelieve and
in the barely-contained rage felt by the country gentleman
in *The Demi-Gods*, is enlarged upon in the stories which bring
out the ambivalent reactions of Conachúr, Ailill, Fuamnach,
Uct Dealv, and Midir. Other emotions — envy, rage, love,
pride — are also examined meticulously yet sympathetically.
By adding these observations of human emotion to the legends'
other-worldly aspects of time, space, and shape, Stephens once
more combines reality and fantasy, making a strange and exotic
world familiar and a very human and age-old situation at
once intriguing and new. His decision to write no more novels
was an unfortunate one for his readers as well as himself,
but these five works mark him as a master of his craft.

If a psychological analysis is one of Stephens' preoccupations
as a modern writer, another is instruction — what the Victorian
novelist might provide in the way of a moral lesson, perhaps,
but more like the instruction envisioned as being given by
the avatars of Theosophical belief. The lessons, whatever they
may be called, are clear. Whether the stories are told by colorful
country folk on the roads of Ireland or by clerks who have
spent their life in Dublin offices, the message is that the breakdown in human communication needs to be healed by loving
kindness. According to Stephens, relationships based on hierarchal structure lead to greed and exploitation on the part of
the employers, a lack of communal spirit or sense of purpose
on the part of workers. This breakdown has occurred along
socio-economic, not nationalistic, lines. The *seoinins*, the believers
in British conservatism, materialism, repressive laws, and government, are members of the Irish middle class; their victims,

usually the weak and the helpless, are the Irish poor. It is
not businessmen alone whom Stephens faults; the "people of
the Fomor" in *The Crock of Gold* include doctors, lawyers, and
professors, the professional class whose services are rarely available to the poor.

A similarly impenetrable and inhumane schism exists also
between husbands and wives, but this conflict is not drawn
along class lines. Quarreling partners range from country folk
to landed gentry, from clerks and their wives to kings and
queens. The message is not dissimilar, however. It is the desire
to possess another, possessiveness of a person's body or mind,
which causes the problem and which often leads to other vices.
Patsy Mac Cann, for example, is insistent upon Mary Mac
Cann's obedience and Eileen Ni Cooley's complete attention,
but he is also greedy for gold; he cannot develop into an
understanding parent and a giving person until he returns
the money he has received from stealing the angels' belongings.
Love transforms Patsy as it changes the Thin Woman, Caitilin,
and Deirdre.

Oliver Gogarty reports Stephens' test for measuring success.
"The point is: how many men have loved you? Women, yes;
but I am not talking about sexual love. How many men have
loved you?"[12] Stephens was fortunate in his male friends. Arthur
Griffith, Thomas Bodkin, AE, Stephen MacKenna, James Joyce,
Samuel Koteliansky changed his life and career in many ways,
and he loved them. But he also loved women, children, animals,
and Ireland, in what seem to be equal amounts.

In his best works, Stephens' love is for every creature and
he displays this affection time and time again. All of his heroines
are motivated by love in its manifold forms — maternal, charitable, sexual, marital. The secret of his successful works is
that in them he embodies love; the later, more arid works
only talk about it. In his last poems he no longer seeks Love
the Magician; he is himself magician, dealing in mystical symbols, esoteric rites, mysterious rituals. Poetry is no longer a
manifestation of love; it comes from the poet's Will. The vitality
one senses in the clash of emotions in *Insurrections*, *The Demi-Gods*,
and *Deirdre* has vanished; whatever energy is left comes from
idiosyncratic punctuation and capitalization.

Perhaps Stephens could be better viewed as juggler than
acrobat. In his best works he balances groups of two, three,

or four characters in order to illustrate certain themes: the Contraries, sexual jealousy, and the divided self. These matters are also encompassed by the theme of love because fulfillment can only come through union. Consider the complex theme of the division of Man which Stephens has said that he envisioned in *The Crock of Gold*. The Philosopher, the Thin Woman, Pan, and Angus Óg represent those aspects of man Blake called the Four Zoas: thought, emotion, the body, divine imagination; the children and the leprecauns represent innocence and "the elemental side of man." At the end of the book, elements of the divided self are united by their affection for each other. Husband and wife, shepherdess and god, children and leprecauns are joined in love and friendship. Only Pan, the lustful foreign god, is without love. Another example of the divided self — the four demi-gods and four humans found in Stephens' third novel — are recombined, through love or its obverse hate, into groups of twos, Finaun and Caeltia, Patsy and Eileen, Mary and Art, even Brien O'Brien and Cuchulain.

If four characters are used to illustrate how the divided self can be united through love, three characters are the way in which Stephens explores sexual jealousy. But the human triangles cannot last indefinitely. In every case love determines the choice which must be made. The stockbroker's wife chooses romance over comfort, Mary Makebelieve chooses vitality over stolidity, Caitilin chooses divine love over lust. Becfola must choose between Dermod and Crimthann, Deirdre between Conachúr and Naoise, Midir between Fuamnach and Etain; but the ultimate triangle is the story of Etain in which she chooses three times: between Dermod and Midir, between Eochaid and Ailill, and between Eochaid and Midir.

Stephens often presents two characters who represent those embattled Contraries, Female Emotion and Male Thought, for example, Mrs. Cafferty and her husband, the Thin Woman and the Philosopher, Eileen Ni Cooley and Patsy Mac Cann, and Maeve and Conachúr. Love often reconciles the warring parties, or it stays the combat when it appears in the form of youthful romance, for instance, Mary and her lodger, Mary Mac Cann and Art, Deirdre and Naoise.

Stephens experiments with the language as well as the characters of love, starting with a modest love poem, "Slán Leath," and moving to both serious and comic conversations on love in *Here Are Ladies*, and his novels. Everything from endearments in the Gaelic fashion to translations of Sappho's love lyrics are of interest to him.

His works are all variations on this theme. Love is the motivation for patriotic essays and adaptations of Gaelic legends; it is the subject of stories concerning husbands and wives, parents and children, man and nature's creations. What shines through the prescriptions for a better world, the psychological analyses, the tales of the fantastic, the romantic, the grotesque, and the realistic is his first, his final, his over-arching theme — love. Stephens' works are his variations on this theme, his valentines to the world.

Notes and References

1 STEPHENS: THE MAN, THE WRITER, THE ENIGMA

1. "An Interview with Mr. James Stephens," by James Esse. *The Irish Statesman* (22 Sep 1923) 48. Stephens used this pseudonym on more than one occasion.
2. Birgit Bramsbäck, *James Stephens: A Literary and Bibliographical Study* (Uppsala: A. B. Lundequistska Bokhandeln, 1959) pp. 16, 19; George Brandon Saul, "Withdrawn in Gold," *Arizona Quarterly*, 9 (1953) 115. Mary Colum expressed doubts that Joyce and Stephens were born in the same year; *Life and the Dream* (Garden City: Doubleday, 1947) p. 392. Norah Hoult gave Stephens' birth date as 1883; Hilde Poepping stated that it was 1884. "James Stephens," *Irish Writing*, No. 27 (June 1954) 55; *James Stephens: Eine Untersuchung über die Irische Erneuerungsbewegung in der Zeit von 1900–1930* (Halle/Saale: N. Niemeyer, 1940) p. 22.
3. Stanley Kunitz (ed.), *Twentieth Century Authors*, 1st supp. (New York: H. W. Wilson, 1955) p. 956. Stephens had made this remark about himself in a speech in 1935 published in a Royal Literary Fund pamphlet.
4. Hilary Pyle, *James Stephens: His Work and an Account of His Life* (London: Routledge & Kegan Paul, 1965) pp. 4–5; L. G. Wickham Legg and E. T. Williams (eds), *Dictionary of National Biography* (London: Oxford University Press, 1959) p. 834.
5. Richard J. Finneran (ed.), *Letters of James Stephens* (London: Macmillan, 1974) pp. 417–19. Hereafter cited as *Letters*.
6. George Moore, '*Hail and Farewell!*': *Vale* (London: William Heinemann, 1914) p. 237.
7. The broadsides were: *Where the Demons Grin* (1908), *Why Thomas Cam Was Grumpy* (1909), *The Adventures of Seumas Beg: The Visit from Abroad* (1910), *The Adventures of Seumas Beg: In the Orchard* (1910), *The Adventures of Seumas Beg: Treasure Trove* (1910), and *The Spy* (1910).

8. AE as quoted by Katharine Tynan in *The Years of the Shadow* (London: Constable, 1919) p. 24. According to MacKenna, the "three Giants of Dublin talk" were Ernest Boyd, Edmund Curtis, and James Stephens. E. R. Dodds (ed.), *Journal and Letters of Stephen MacKenna* (London: Constable, 1936) p. 148.

9. Adapted from the Fenian cycle are "The Boyhood of Fionn," "The Birth of Bran," "Oisín's Mother," "The Little Brawl at Allen," "The Carl of the Drab Coat," and "The Enchanted Cave of Cesh Corran." "The Story of Tuan Mac Cairill" is mythological; "The Wooing of Becfola," "Becuma of the White Skin," and "Mongan's Frenzy" are historical, although there are mythological components to all three tales.

10. *In the Land of Youth* also contains two mythological tales, "The Dream of Angus" and "The Tale of the Two Swineherds," and a story which is both historical and mythological, "The Wooing of Etain."

11. Preface written by Stephens to *The Poetical Works of Thomas MacDonagh* (Dublin: Talbot Press, 1916) pp. ix–x.

12. Alan Denson (ed.), *Letters from AE* (London: Abelard-Schuman, 1961) pp. 167, 171.

13. Quoted by Oliver St. John Gogarty in "James Stephens," *Colby Library Quarterly*, 5 (Mar 1961) 211.

14. Norah Hoult, "James Stephens," 57.

15. B. L. Reid, *The Man from New York: John Quinn and His Friends* (New York: Oxford University Press, 1968) offers details on the relationship between Quinn and Stephens. See, for example, pp. 70, 162–3, 197, 318, 319, 431–2, 489–90.

16. Howe's letters to Harris are held in the Henry W. and Albert A. Berg Collection, New York Public Library. Hereafter cited as the Berg Collection.

17. Letter to Patricia McFate from Jane Novak dated 22 Feb 1969.

18. Resource books on the Irish Literary Revival include the following which are listed in the Selected Bibliography: Ernest Boyd, *Ireland's Literary Renaissance*; Blanche Kelly, *The Voice of the Irish*; and Lloyd Morris, *The Celtic Dawn*. Also see Herbert Howarth, *The Irish Writers* (London: Rockliff, 1958) and Richard J. Loftus, *Nationalism in Modern Anglo-Irish Poetry* (Madison: University of Wisconsin Press, 1964).

19. Yeats's interest in Theosophy, the Hermetic Society, and other spiritual pursuits is recorded in Richard Ellmann, *Yeats: The Man and the Masks* (New York: Macmillan, 1948) pp. 41–3, 56–69, 86–98, 121–2.

20. *Letters from AE*, p. 17. Russell stated that the two influences on his mystical thought and writing were Madame Blavatsky and the sacred books of the East. This contention is quoted twice in Abinash Chandra Bose, *Three Mystic Poets* (Kolhapur, India: Kolhapur School and College Bookstall, 1945) pp. 69, 79–80. For his contemporaries' remarks on AE's visions and occult interests, see W. B. Yeats, *Autobiographies* (London: Macmillan, 1926) p. 299; Darrell Figgis, *A. E. (George W. Russell): A Study of a Man and a Nation* (Dublin: Maunsel, 1916) p. 29; and James Stephens, "AE:I," in Lloyd Frankenberg (ed.), *James, Seumas and Jacques: Unpublished Writings of James Stephens* (London: Macmillan, 1964) pp. 111–12.

21. George Moore, '*Hail and Farewell!*': *Vale*, p. 165.
22. These quotations are taken from Edward Martyn, "A Plea for the Revival of the Irish Literary Theatre," *Irish Review*, 4 (Apr 1914) 79, 83.
23. *Sinn Féin* (7 May 1910).
24. Stephens edited Moore's drafts of the first three stories in *A Story-Teller's Holiday*. In May 1917 Moore wrote Stephens: "I think that if you will correct my mistakes and sprinkle the idiom over the story ... crossing out any of my sentences you like if the omission will help you in your editing, you will have accomplished the end I have in view." Quoted in Joseph Hone, *The Life of George Moore* (London: Gollancz, 1936) p. 336.
25. Richard Ellmann (ed.), *Letters of James Joyce* (New York: Viking, 1966) 2, p. 260.
26. *James, Seumas and Jacques*, p. 149.
27. For Stephens' early comments on Joyce, see *Letters*, pp. 138-9, 155, 209, 221, 233, 282-3.
28. Stuart Gilbert (ed.), *Letters of James Joyce* (New York: Viking, 1957) I, pp. 253-4, 282, 288.
29. James Joyce, "Continuation of a Work in Progress," *transition*, 8 (Nov 1927) 30.
30. *Letters of James Joyce*, I, p. 282; Stephens' other remark is quoted by Padraic Colum in his Preface to Lloyd Frankenberg (ed.), *A James Stephens Reader* (New York: Macmillan, 1962) p. xix.
31. Beatrice, Lady Glenavy, *Today We Will Only Gossip* (London: Constable, 1964) pp. 180-1.
32. *Letters*, p. 407. Richard Finneran suggests that "D" is probably Dilys Powell, the English critic.
33. *Today We Will Only Gossip*, p. 182.
34. *James, Seumas and Jacques*, pp. 70, 109, 149, 164.
35. "A Rhinoceros, Some Ladies, and a Horse," *James, Seumas and Jacques*, pp. 3-15.
36. Austin Clarke, *A Penny in the Clouds* (London: Routledge & Kegan Paul, 1968) pp. 109-10. Birgit Bramsbäck, *James Stephens: A Literary and Bibliographical Study*, p. 15. *James, Seumas and Jacques*, pp. 28-33 (an autobiographical sketch).
37. Lennox Robinson (ed.), *Lady Gregory's Journals, 1916-1930*, (Dublin: Putnam, 1946) p. 267. *Letters from AE*, p. 65; Moore's remarks are in *Vale* and elsewhere; Robinson's speculation is frequently heard in Dublin.
38. "The Old Woman's Money," *Century Magazine*, 90 (May 1915) 49; "An Essay in Cubes," *English Review*, 17 (Apr 1914) 83.
39. *Letters*, p. 205.
40. Manuscript belonging to Iris Wise.
41. *Irish Fairy Tales* (London: Macmillan, 1920) p. 63.
42. *A Penny in the Clouds*, p. 109.
43. Undated note in the Berg Collection; postcard belonging to Iris Wise.
44. Quoted by Sir William Rothenstein in *Since Fifty: Men and Memories, 1922-1938* (New York: Macmillan, 1940) pp. 86-7.
45. David Marcus, "One Afternoon with James Stephens," *Irish Writing*,

No. 14 (Mar 1951) 44; Arthur Moss, "James Stephens," *Bookman*, 56 (Jan 1923) 596; Blanche Kelly, *The Voice of the Irish* (New York: Sheed & Ward, 1952) p. 246; Ernest A. Boyd, *Portraits: Real and Imaginary* (New York: George H. Doran, 1924) p. 246. Also see George Brandon Saul, "On Mercury and Reason: The Criticism of James Stephens," in *Stephens, Yeats, and Other Irish Concerns* (New York: New York Public Library, 1954) p. 37; and Edward Roberts, "An Evening with James Stephens," *Dalhousie Review*, 32 (Spring 1952) 55.

2   THE DANCE OF LIFE

1. *On Prose and Verse* (New York: Bowling Green Press, 1928) p. 18.
2. *On Prose*, p. 18.
3. *On Prose*, p. 23.
4. *On Prose*, p. 23.
5. *On Prose*, p. 27.
6. The schema may be followed in the second and third novels. Although Caitilin Ni Murrachu's hair is not described, the stormy-natured girl who loves Mac Culain has black hair. While the kindly Angus Og has golden ringlets, the temperamental Pan has brown curls. Patsy Mac Cann's hair is dark; his daughter's hair is fair.
7. *Arthur Griffith: Journalist and Statesman* (Dublin: Wilson, Hartnell, 1922) p. 12.
8. Sir William Rothenstein speaks of Stephens' claim that "all Dublin policemen were created by Praxiteles." *Since Fifty*, p. 88.
9. *The Charwoman's Daughter* (London: Macmillan, 1912) pp. 65–6.
10. It was first published in *Sinn Féin*, (6 Nov 1909).
11. *The Charwoman's Daughter*, pp. 115–16.
12. *The Charwoman's Daughter*, p. 131.
13. ". . . he could love her better after punishing her. . . ." "He saw none but Clara, hated none, loved none, save the intolerable woman." (Westminster: Constable, 1897) pp. 196, 231. Clara's hair with its "irreclaimable curls" is similar to that of Mary's, and Crossjay Patterne, who has never had enough to eat "in his life," is surely related to the lodger. Cornelius Weygandt mentions aspects of the influence of Meredith on Stephens' works in *The Time of Yeats* (New York: D. Appleton-Century, 1937) pp. 219–20.
14. *Sinn Féin* (11 May 1907).
15. Oscar Wilde, *A House of Pomegranates* (Leipzig: B. Tauchnitz, 1909) pp. 23–4.
16. *The Charwoman's Daughter*, p. 188.
17. The manuscript is in the Berg Collection.
18. *The Charwoman's Daughter*, p. 225.
19. *Here Are Ladies*, p. 83.
20. *The Charwoman's Daughter*, p. 224; *The Crock of Gold* (London: Macmillan, 1912) p. 150.

21. This reading of the novel as a cohesive work of art refutes the opinions of other critics, for example, H. P. Marshall who finds the book "baffling" because it is "without a tangible ending," and George E. Hatvary who believes that "it is not design but lack of it that tends to distinguish *The Crock of Gold* from other novels." "James Stephens," *London Mercury*, 12 (Sep 1925) 503; "Re-reading 'The Crock of Gold,'" *Irish Writing*, No. 22 (Mar 1953) p. 63.
22. *The Crock of Gold*, p. 30.
23. "[For Stephens] understanding of Life is achieved only in the degree that life is experienced, and the sole open sesame to existence lies in keenness of perception and sensitiveness of intuition. To live adequately is to realize, emotionally and intellectually, the widest range of experience that life offers to the individual, and to hold the spirit open to the dynamic force of change." Lloyd R. Morris, *The Celtic Dawn: A Survey of the Renascence in Ireland, 1889-1916* (New York: Macmillan, 1917) p. 190.
24. The son of Cumhail was Fionn, another great warrior.
25. Robert Shafer, for example, finds the stories "..ill-timed sermons . . . spoiling such an otherwise wholly delightful tale." "James Stephens and the Poetry of the Day," *Forum*, 50 (Oct 1913) 567.
26. For further discussions of this topic, see: Hazard Adams, *Blake and Yeats: The Contrary Vision* (Ithaca: Cornell University Press, 1955); Northrop Frye, "Yeats and the Language of Symbolism," *University of Toronto Quarterly*, 17 (Oct 1947) 1-17; Hilary Pyle, *James Stephens: His Work and an Account of His Life*; Margaret Rudd, *Divided Image: A Study of William Blake and W. B. Yeats* (London: Routledge & Kegan Paul, 1953).
27. Stephens used this expression in a letter to Edward Marsh dated Feb 1914. *Letters*, p. 121.
28. William Blake, 'The Argument', *The Marriage of Heaven and Hell*.
29. *Sinn Féin* (5 Oct 1907); *Sinn Féin* (7 May 1910).
30. "An Essay in Cubes," *English Review*, 17 (Apr 1914) 93.
31. In a review of *The Wisdom of the West*, by James H. Cousins. *Irish Review*, 2 (April 1912) 101.
32. *The Demi-Gods* (London: Macmillan, 1914) p. 54.
33. "William Blake," in *James, Seumas and Jacques*, pp. 199-200.
34. *The Crock of Gold*, p. 12.
35. *The Crock of Gold*, p. 164.
36. *English review*, 17 (Apr 1914) 93.
37. *The Crock of Gold*, p. 153.
38. *The Crock of Gold*, p. 163.
39. Review of *The Wisdom of the West*, p. 102.
40. "A Descriptive Catalogue," in David V. Erdman (ed.), *The Poetry and Prose of William Blake* (Garden City: Doubleday, 1965) p. 533.
41. *The Crock of Gold*, p. 302. In his essay, "Poetry," Stephens made a similar union. "The wisdom of the serpent cannot be allied to the harmlessnes [sic] of the dove, but the wisdom of a wise man can be allied to the artlessness of a child . . .," *Sinn Féin* (22 June 1907).
42. "When I was a youngster I used to do an odd trick: maybe we all

do it. I used to squat beside the dog or the cat, or beside a cow or a bird, and try to 'be' myself into the being of that creature. I used to moo at the cow and whistle at the bird and they always answered back. You could see them listening to the sounds you made, and you could see them being highly pleased at being taken notice of." "Living — Whatever That Is," in *James, Seumas and Jacques*, p. 265.

43. Stephens praises dancing as "freedom in excess" in "Irish Idiosyncrasies," *Sinn Féin* (7 May 1910). The Old Philosopher enlarges on dancers and non-dancers in "There is a Tavern in the Town — II," *Here Are Ladies*, p. 287.

44. Augustine Martin, "The Short Stories of James Stephens," *Colby Library Quarterly*, 6 (Dec 1963) 344.

45. Anatole France, *La Révolte des Anges* (Paris: Calmann-Levy, 1914).

46. "In the Poppy Field" and "Mac Dhoul," which were printed in the *Irish Review* in March 1911 and January 1912, appear in *The Hill of Vision*. That collection also contains "Nucleolus" and "Mount Derision," two poems on male-female conflict which are related to Finaun's tale; "The Fulness of Time," in which the magician's Regent, Uriel, appears; and "The Brute," concerning the collapse of a man during an argument with a woman, a poem which recalls Patsy's quarrel with Eileen.

47. *Kings and the Moon* (London: Macmillan, 1938) p. 5.

48. "Irish Tinkers or 'Travellers,' " *Béaloideas*, 3 (Dec 1931) 174.

49. "On His Poems: IV," in *James, Seumas and Jacques*, p. 227.

50. *The Demi-Gods*, p. 47.

51. *The Charwoman's Daughter*, pp. 42–3.

52. William Y. Tindall, *Forces in Modern British Literature* (New York: A. A. Knopf, 1947) p. 98.

53. *La Révolte des Anges*, p. 112.

54. *The Demi-Gods*, pp. 129, 157, 203–4.

55. *The Demi-Gods*, pp. 56–7.

56. A sketchy outline for a three-act play of *The Charwoman's Daughter* is extant.

57. *James Stephens*, p. 63.

58. The draft is written on notebook paper available to Stephens only in his capacity as Registrar of the National Gallery of Ireland, a post he held after the publication of the novel. The manuscript is in the Berg Collection. The typescript belongs to Iris Wise. The typescript has been edited by Richard Finneran and published in *The Journal of Irish Literature*, 4 (Sep 1975) 10–46.

59. *Letters*, p. 159.

60. The letter is postmarked 4 December 1930. Allan Wade (ed.), *The Letters of W. B. Yeats* (London: R. Hart-Davis, 1954) p. 780.

61. Ernest Boyd, *Ireland's Literary Renaissance* (Dublin and London: Maunsel, 1916) p. 393.

62. *Letters*, pp. 159, 201. Stephens did tell Stephen MacKenna that *The Demi-Gods* was "not as good as The Crock, but then I had the subject there & I hadn't here." *Letters*, p. 144.

63. Even one of his most enthusiastic critics, Birgit Bramsbäck, finds it "surprising that Stephens should have thought so highly of *The Demi-*

Gods." "James Stephens: Dublin — Paris — Return," *Colby Library Quarterly*, 5 (Mar 1961) 217.

3 THE QUEST THAT DESTINY COMMANDS

1. Typescript in the Berg Collection.
2. "Unity," p. 22.
3. In a letter dated 1 March 1911 to Stephen MacKenna, Stephens announced that he was going to appear in a Gaelic play, *Bairbre Ruadh* ("Redhaired Barbara"), written by Padraic O Conaire. "I think it is a very good way of getting quick Gaelic. Seagdan Óg also comes to lecture me & I have great hopes now of climbing to the austere heights from which one may declaim Gaelic verse & know what its about." *Letters*, p. 23.
4. *Letters*, p. 61.
5. *Letters*, p. 114.
6. *Letters*, p. 256. On 2 July 1913, he had sent a sample story to Howe claiming "it is not precisely on the lines you wish, but is very close to it, &, from it, you can judge whether my stuff would please the youngsters you have in mind." *Letters*, p. 64. Whatever the reason, a volume of Stephens' "Children's Stories" did not materialize.
7. Both typescripts are in the Berg Collection.
8. Autographed copy of *Irish Fairy Tales* (London: Macmillan, 1920) presented by Stephens to Howe. In the Berg Collection.
9. Lennox Robinson (ed.), *Lady Gregory's Journals, 1916–1930* (Dublin: Putnam, 1946) p. 268.
10. This tale is told in several Gaelic manuscripts, the earliest being The Book of the Dun Cow. It was published in English as an Appendix to the second volume of *The Voyage of Bran* (London: David Nutt, 1897) by Kuno Meyer, who constructed his text from the Dun Cow, and the Rawlinson, Betham, and Harleian manuscripts, dating from the fourteenth, fifteenth, and sixteenth centuries. Appendix A, pp. 294–301.
11. *Irish Fairy Tales*, p. 16.
12. *Letters*, pp. 260, 259. He also recommended "Tuan" to Henry McBride, John Quinn, and John Houston Finley: *Letters*, pp. 257, 258, 276.
13. Contemporary translations of the stories which were available to Stephens included "The Boyish Exploits of Finn," *Ériu*, 1 (1904) 180–90, and Standish Hayes O'Grady (ed. and trans.), "The Colloquy with the Ancients," *Silva Gadelica* (London and Edinburgh: Williams and Norgate, 1892) 2, pp. 101–265.
14. *Irish Fairy Tales*, p. 66.
15. Lady Gregory tells versions of the Bran and Oisín stories in *Gods and Fighting Men* (London: John Murray, 1904) pp. 172–8.
16. A translation of the story was also produced by Patrick Kennedy in *Legendary Fictions of the Irish Celts* (London and New York: Benjamin Blom, 1891) pp. 207–11.

17. *Silva Gadelica*, 1, pp. 85–7; 2, pp. 91–3. According to James Carney, the Becfola story is another adaptation of the primitive Tristan-Iseult legend in which there is a substitution for the navigational portion of the tale, and the union of the lovers is postponed until the matter of the young man's career is settled. He dates the original tale as about A.D. 900. See *Studies in Irish Literature and History* (Dublin: Dublin Institute for Advanced Studies, 1955) pp. 195, 229–30.
18. The Gaelic sagas and their translations may be found in *Silva Gadelica*: 1, pp. 336–42; 2, pp. 378–85 ("The little Brawl at Almhain").
1, pp. 289–96; 2, pp. 324–31 ("The Carle of the Drab Coat").
1, pp. 306–10; 2, pp. 343–7 ("The Enchanted Cave of Keshcorran").
19. *Irish Fairy Tales*, pp. 198–9.
20. *Irish Fairy Tales*, pp. 205–6.
21. A version of the first tale, as translated by R. I. Best, is found in "The Adventures of Art Son of Conn, and the Courtship of Delbchaem," *Ériu*, 3 (1907) 149–73. This and a related tale concerning Mongan are translated by Kuno Meyer in Vol. 1 of *The Voyage of Bran* (London: David Nutt, 1895) pp. 56–84.
22. Geoffrey Keating, *The History of Ireland*, Rev. Patrick S. Dinneen (ed. and trans.) (London: David Nutt, 1908) 2, pp. 190–7. Douglas Hyde, *A Literary History of Ireland* (London: T. Fisher Unwin, 1899) pp. 302–18.
23. *The Insurrection in Dublin* (Dublin: Maunsel, 1916) p. 31.
24. *Deirdre* (London: Macmillan, 1923) p. 285.
25. Note pasted in Howe's copy of *Deirdre*. In the Berg Collection.
26. Letter pasted in Howe's copy of *Deirdre*. In the Berg Collection.
27. James Carney, *Studies in Irish Literature and History*, pp. 217–20, 232–7.
28. *Deirdre*, p. 155.
29. *A Literary History of Ireland*, p. 298.
30. *Letters*, p. 292. Stephens was pleased with his work, writing John Quinn that it was "easily the best thing I have ever done," a remark which he repeated with even more enthusiasm in a letter to W. T. H. Howe: "it is the best ever, and, more than that, it is better than the best ever." *Letters*, pp. 263, 288.
31. Dorothy Hoare, *The Works of Morris and Yeats in Relation to Early Saga Literature* (Cambridge: Cambridge University Press, 1937) p. 134.
32. It was edited and translated by Kuno Meyer in *Revue Celtique*, 10 (Apr 1889) 212–28; 11 (Jan 1890) 209–10.
33. *Revue Celtique*, 10 (April 1889) 215.
34. *Revue Celtique*, 10 (April 1889) 217.
35. "Two Irish Tales," *Revue Celtique*, 3 (Jan and Nov 1878) 347.
36. Letter pasted in Howe's copy of *Deirdre*. In the Berg Collection.
37. Letter pasted in Howe's copy of *In the Land of Youth*. In the Berg Collection.
38. *The Works of Morris and Yeats in Relation to Early Saga Literature*, pp. 136, 138–9.

4 MAKE IT SING/MAKE IT NEW

1. Letter to W. T. H. Howe, *Letters*, p. 65.
2. Randall Jarrell, "Recent Poetry," *Yale Review*, 44 (Summer 1955) 600.

3. *Letters*, p. 17.
4. *Letters*, p. 15.
5. Letter to Lewis Chase, *Letters*, p. 202.
6. *Insurrections* (Dublin: Maunsel, 1909) pp. 21–3.
7. *Insurrections*, p. 7.
8. *Letters*, p. 169.
9. For a discussion of Stephens' exploration of childhood in *The Crock of Gold*, see Ch. 2. For an example of harsh critical response, see Crawford Neil's book review, "Little Jimmie (alias Seumas Beg)" in *New Ireland* (4 Dec 1915) pp. 62–3.
10. *The Adventures of Seumas Beg/The Rocky Road to Dublin* (London: Macmillan, 1915) p. 54. Hereafter cited as *Rocky Road*.
11. *Rocky Road*, p. 74.
12. *Letters of James Joyce*, p. 317. Joyce believed that he and Stephens were born on the same day, 2 Feb 1882.
13. *Letters*, p. 371.
14. *The Hill of Vision* (Dublin: Maunsel, 1912) pp. 7, 9.
15. *The Hill of Vision*, p. 28.
16. *The Hill of Vision*, p. 46.
17. He made this claim to Kees Van Hock. See "The Man Who Invented Glocca Mora," *The Irish Digest* (Nov 1950) 51. For a further discussion of the influence of Blake's writings, see Ch. 2.
18. He speaks about *Songs of Innocence* in a lecture given on the BBC, "On His Poems: III," *James, Seumas and Jacques*, pp. 220–1. Also see Barton R. Friedman, "William Blake to James Stephens: The Crooked Road," *Éire-Ireland*, 1 (Fall 1966) 29–57.
19. Letter dated 21 July 1957. Quoted in *Letters from AE*, p. 231.
20. *Letters*, p. 121.
21. *Letters*, p. 123.
22. *Letters*, p. 174.
23. Autographed book in the Berg Collection. A letter written on a page of the book is dated 21 Dec 1916.
24. Autographed book in the Berg Collection.
25. *Letters*, p. 179.
26. Letter to James Stephens dated March 1915. *Letters from AE*, pp. 102–3.
27. *Letters*, pp. 218–19.
28. See *Letters*, p. 237, for Stephens' explanation of the title to Sir Frederick Macmillan. Stephens explained his technique to John Quinn: "It ['The Coolun'] also I pinched from Raftery, that is, I hooked one line out of the decent man's Irish, and I played on that line the way Pan plays on his pipes, only better." *Letters*, pp. 223–4. In his "Note" in *Reincarnations*, Stephens divides the poems into three groups according to his method: translation, creation of a poem around "a phrase, a line, half a line," and paraphrase of subject matter without regard to the original arrangement of material. *Reincarnations* (London: Macmillan, 1918) pp. 61–2.
29. Douglas Hyde (ed.), *The Love Songs of Connacht, Being the Fourth Chapter of the Songs of Connacht* (Dundrum: Dun Emer Press, 1904). Douglas Hyde (ed.), *Songs Ascribed to Raftery, Being the Fifth Chapter of the Songs*

of Connacht (Baile atha Cliath: Gill agus a mac, 1903). Patrick S. Dinneen and Tadgh O'Donoghue (eds), *The Poems of Egan O'Rahilly* (London: David Nutt, 1911) [*Irish Texts Society*, Vol. 3]. John C. Mac Erlean (ed.), *The Poems of David O'Bruadair*, 3 vols. (London: David Nutt, 1913) [*Irish Texts Society*, Vols. 11, 13, 18]. His source for the other poems was *Collected Works of Padraic H. Pearse: Songs of the Irish Rebels and Specimens from an Irish Anthology* (Dublin & London: Maunsel, 1918). For an excellent study in depth of Stephens' use of his sources, see Richard J. Finneran, "The Sources of James Stephens's *Reincarnations*: 'Alone I Did It, Barring for the Noble Assistance of the Gods,'" *Tulane Studies in English*, 22 (1977) 143–53.

30. *The Love Songs of Connacht*, pp. 55–6.
31. *Reincarnations*, pp. 4–5.
32. *Letters*, pp. 231, 232. The misspelling of "gorgeous" is Stephens'.
33. These rules have been recorded by Myles Dillon in *Early Irish Literature* (Chicago: University of Chicago Press, 1948) pp. 176–7.
34. Douglas Hyde, *A Literary History of Ireland*, p. 531.
35. *Reincarnations*, p. 1.
36. *Reincarnations*, pp. 64–5.
37. *Letters*, p. 277. His liking of this poem is reflected in his dedication of the work to Howe.
38. *Letters*, pp. 338–9.
39. Two editions, a New York and a London one, were published in 1925 with slightly differing order and content. A new edition, dated 1926, added a foreword and seven poems to the 1925 American version. The new poems were: "Little Things," "The Snare," "The Merry Music," "The Fifteen Acres," "The Crest Jewel," "Thy Soul," and "Christmas in Freelands."
40. *A Poetry Recital* (London: Macmillan, 1925) p. 15.
41. *James, Seumas and Jacques*, p. 179.
42. *Songs from the Clay* (New York: Macmillan, 1915) p. 25.
43. *Collected Poems* (London: Macmillan, 1926) pp. 3–4.
44. *Songs from the Clay*, p. 1.
45. *Collected Poems*, p. 16.
46. Poems which might serve as examples of the subject matter are, in order and by section of *Collected Poems*: "The Goat Paths," "The Fifteen Acres," "The Lark," "The Snare," "Little Things"; "To the Queen of the Bees," "The Canal Bank," "The Daisies," "The End of the Road," "The Girl I Left Behind Me," "The Watcher," "Nora Criona"; "The Piper," "Hesperus," "The Paps of Dana," "This Way to Winter," "White Fields," "Etched in Frost"; "Seumas Beg," "Breakfast Time," "The Apple Tree," "The White Window"; "The Weavers," "The Street Behind Yours," "A Street," "Fifty Pounds a Year and a Pension"; "The Breath of Life," "On a Reed," "The Rose on the Wind," "The Merry Music," "The Crest Jewel," "Thy Soul," and "The Pit of Bliss."
47. *Letters*, p. 330.
48. *Collected Poems*, pp. xii–xiii.
49. *On Prose and Verse* (New York: Bowling Green Press, 1928) pp. 13, 33, 35. Stephens took a similar stand in his commentary in *English*

Romantic Poets, a volume he co-edited with Edwin L. Beck and Royall H. Snow. "Every story is situated in time: no poem is. . . . Every story is incomplete: no poem is. Therefore prose values are at the mercy of the next day: poetic values are only at the mercy of the language." (New York: American Book Co., 1933) p. xxi.

50. *Theme and Variations* (New York: Fountain Press, 1930) p. 25. The poem, "Theme and Variations," also appears in modified and expanded form in *Strict Joy*.
51. *Theme and Variations*, p. 16.
52. *Theme and Variations*, p. 20.
53. *Kings and the Moon* (London: Macmillan, 1938) p. 1.
54. *Kings and the Moon*, p. 72.

5 THE ART AND CRAFT OF PROSE

1. *Letters*, p. 17.
2. *Letters*, p. 61.
3. *Letters*, p. 204.
4. The essays contributed to *The Crock of Gold* were: "On Washing," "On Going to Bed," and "The Old Philosopher Discourses on Policemen." Those rewritten for *Here Are Ladies* were: "On Shaving," "On Eating," "On Drinking," "The Old Philosopher: James Stephens' Mentor Discusses Smoking and Incidentally the Budget," "The Old Philosopher: The Thoughts of Englishmen," "The Old Philosopher: Considers Legs and Wheels," "The Old Philosopher: Talks of the Absurdity of Marriage," "The Old Philosopher: Discourses on Education," "The Old Philosopher: Discourses on the North Pole," "The Old Philosopher: Discourses on Language," "The Old Philosopher: Discourses on Poetry," and "On Dancing."
5. They are entitled, "The Old Philosopher: Discourses on the Viceregal Microbe," "The Old Philosopher: Discourses on Government," and "On Lawyers." They are reprinted in the James Stephens issue of *The Journal of Irish Literature*, 4 (Sep 1975) 55–61, 63–5.
6. Rewritten for *Here Are Ladies* were: "Mrs. Jerry Gorman" ("Three Angry People: II"); "Miss Arabella Hennessy" ("Three Women Who Wept: III"); "Mrs. Larry Tracy" ("Three Women Who Wept: II"); "Miss Kathleen Raftery" ("Three Young Wives: II"); "Mr. Aloysius Murphy" ("Three Lovers Who Lost: III"); "Mrs. Bernard Nagle" ("Three Young Wives: I"); and "Mr. John Monroe" ("Three Heavy Husbands: III"). "The Unworthy Princess," a short story published in the *Irish Homestead*, became "Three Lovers Who Lost: II." Eleven stories reworked for the volume originally appeared in *The Nation*: "A Heavy Husband" ("Three Heavy Husbands: II"); "The Young Man Out of a Book" ("Three Women Who Wept: I"); "Not at Home" ("Three Angry People: III"); "The Triangle" ("Three Heavy Husbands: I"); "The Stone-Man" ("Three Angry People: I"); "The Morning Road" ("Three Happy Places: III"); "By Fire Light" ("Three Young Wives:

III"); "Un Bock Brun" ("A Glass of Beer"); "The Horses"; "The Triangle"; and "The Blind Man." Those adapted for use in *The Crock of Gold* were: "Old Mrs. Hannigan," "The Man Who Was Afraid," and "Grierson's Discovery."

7. *The Journal of Irish Literature*, p. 180.

8. The original scheme of organization is set forth by Stephens in a letter to James B. Pinker, his agent, on 28 March 1913. *Letters*, p. 53. Stephens agreed to add additional stories on 11 April 1913. *Letters*, p. 54.

9. *Here Are Ladies*, pp. 217–18.

10. *Here Are Ladies*, p. 1.

11. *Here Are Ladies*, pp. 38–9.

12. "I was born into the outskirts of a city that was packed with horses . . . . Goodness — there were human beings there also, who looked exactly like horses and said 'Neigh' to everything, and very excellent men — and here and there a woman — who looked exactly like asses and only didn't bray because they were too shy. . . . The Dublin streets that I first knew thudded and neighed and whinnied with every kind of horse that can be imagined, and they also snorted and screamed with kinds of horses that can't now be imagined at all." James Stephens writing on horses in "No More Peasants," *James, Seumas and Jacques*, p. 272.

13. *Here Are Ladies*, p. 105.

14. *Letters*, p. 65.

15. Autographed book in the Berg Collection. A letter from Stephens to Howe pasted in the front of the book is dated 31 May 1913.

16. "Stephens' treatment of the woman character is a dramatization of the age-old paradox, man-propounded, that men can neither live with women or without them." Clarice Short, "James Stephens' Women," *Western Humanities Review*, 10 (1956) 288.

17. *In the Land of Youth*, p. 101.

18. *The Charwoman's Daughter*, p. 127.

19. Letter in the Berg Collection.

20. Stephens praised "Hunger" and "Clair de Lune" (probably an early title for "Etched in Moonlight") in a letter to Harold Loeb dated 14 July 1922. *Letters*, p. 278.

21. "Hunger," *Etched in Moonlight* (New York: Macmillan, 1928) p. 30.

22. "Hunger," p. 42.

23. "Hunger," p. 51.

24. *Letters*, p. 360.

25. Roger Chauviré, *The Sword in the Soul*, trans. Ernest Boyd (London, New York, and Toronto: Longmans Green, 1929) p. viii.

26. *How St. Patrick Saves the Irish* (privately printed, 1931) p. 5.

27. *James, Seumas and Jacques*, p. 3.

28. *James, Seumas and Jacques*, p. x.

29. *James, Seumas and Jacques*, p. 73.

30. *James, Seumas and Jacques*, p. 141.

31. *James, Seumas and Jacques*, p. 156.

32. *James, Seumas and Jacques*, p. 254.

33. *James, Seumas and Jacques*, p. 222.

34. *James, Seumas and Jacques*, p. 121.

6 THE MARRIAGE OF THE CONTRARIES

1. Frank O'Connor, *A Short History of Irish Literature* (New York: G. P. Putnam's Sons, 1967) p. 216.
2. Hilary Pyle, *James Stephens*, p. 174.
3. *Letters from AE*, pp. 71, 74–5.
4. Gerald Dewitt Sanders, John Herbert Nelson, and M. L. Rosenthal (eds.), *Chief Modern Poets of England and America* (New York: Macmillan, 1962) 1, p. 5.
5. Randall Jarrell, "Recent Poetry," *Yale Review*, 44 (Summer 1955) 600.
6. Oliver St. John Gogarty, "James Stephens," *Colby Library Quarterly*, Ser. 5 (Mar 1961) 210.
7. *The Demi-Gods*, pp. 184–5.
8. Richard J. Loftus, *Nationalism in Modern Anglo-Irish Poetry* (Madison: University of Wisconsin Press, 1964) p. 227.
9. "The Novelist and Final Utterance," *Irish Statesman* (12 Apr 1924) p. 140.
10. William Rothenstein speaks of Stephens in 1940 still in love with Ireland: singing old songs, telling legends, and gossiping about Dublin friends. *Since Fifty*, p. 86.
11. "Are you sad, my heart? then keep / Singing, singing, lest you weep." "A reply," *Songs from the Clay*, p. 103.
12. "James Stephens," 205.

Selected Bibliography

PRIMARY SOURCES

Insurrections (Dublin: Maunsel, 1909; New York: Macmillan, 1909)

The Charwoman's Daughter (London: Macmillan, 1912) Identical with *Mary, Mary* (Boston: Small, Maynard, 1912)

The Hill of Vision (New York: Macmillan, 1912; Dublin: Maunsel, 1912)

The Crock of Gold (London: Macmillan, 1912; New York: Macmillan, 1913)

Here Are Ladies (London and New York: Macmillan, 1913)

Five New Poems, Flying Fame Chapbooks, 2nd ser. (London: printed by A. I. Stevens for *Flying Fame*, 1913)

The Demi-Gods (London and New York: Macmillan, 1914)

Songs from the Clay (London and New York: Macmillan, 1915)

The Adventures of Seumas Beg/The Rocky Road to Dublin (London and New York: Macmillan, 1915)

Green Branches (Dublin and London: Maunsel, 1916; New York: Macmillan, 1916)

The Insurrection in Dublin (Dublin and London: Maunsel, 1916; New York: Macmillan, 1916)

Hunger: A Dublin Story [by James Esse] (Dublin: The Candles Press, 1918)

Reincarnations (London and New York: Macmillan, 1918)

Irish Fairy Tales (London and New York: Macmillan, 1920)

Arthur Griffith: Journalist and Statesman (Dublin: Wilson, Hartnell [1922])

The Hill of Vision, 3rd ed. (London: Macmillan, 1922)

Deirdre (London and New York: Macmillan, 1923)

Little Things (Freelands, Ky.: privately printed by W. M. Hill, 1924)

In the Land of Youth (London and New York: Macmillan, 1924)

A Poetry Recital (New York: Macmillan, 1925)

A Poetry Recital (London: Macmillan, 1925)

Christmas in Freelands (Freelands, Ky.: privately printed by W. M. Hill, 1925)

A Poetry Recital, new ed. (New York and London: Macmillan, 1926)

Collected Poems (London and New York: Macmillan, 1926)
Etched in Moonlight (London and New York: Macmillan, 1928)
On Prose and Verse (New York: Bowling Green Press, 1928)
Julia Elizabeth: A Comedy in One Act (New York: Crosby Gaige, 1929)
The Optimist (Gaylordsville, Conn.: Slide Mountain Press, 1929)
The Outcast (London: Faber & Faber, 1929)
Theme and Variations (New York: Fountain Press, 1930)
How St. Patrick Saves the Irish (privately printed, 1931)
Strict Joy (London and New York: Macmillan, 1931)
Stars Do Not Make a Noise (Los Angeles: Deux Magots Press, 1931)
Kings and the Moon (London and New York: Macmillan, 1938)
Collected Poems, 2nd ed. (London and New York: Macmillan, 1954)
A James Stephens Reader, ed. Lloyd Frankenberg (New York: Macmillan, 1962)
James, Seumas and Jacques: Unpublished Writings by James Stephens, ed. Lloyd Frankenberg (London and New York: Macmillan, 1964)
Letters of James Stephens, ed. Richard J. Finneran (London and New York: Macmillan, 1974)

SELECTED SECONDARY SOURCES

Boyd, Ernest, *Ireland's Literary Renaissance* (Dublin and London: Maunsel, 1916)
——, *Portraits: Real and Imaginary* (New York: George H. Doran, 1924)
Bradley, William, "James Stephens: An Appreciation," *Bookman*, 41 (March 1915) 20–2
Bramsbäck, Birgit, "James Stephens: Dublin — Paris — Return," *Colby Library Quarterly*, Ser. 5 (March 1961) 215–24
——, *James Stephens: A Literary and Bibliographical Study* (Uppsala: A. B. Lundequistska Bokhandeln, 1959)
Colum, Padraic, "James Stephens as a Prose Artist," in *A James Stephens Reader*, ed. Lloyd Frankenberg (New York: Macmillan, 1962)
Ellmann, Richard, *James Joyce* (New York: Oxford University Press, 1959)
Finneran, Richard J., "A Further Note on Joyce and Stephens," *James Joyce Quarterly*, 13 (Winter 1976) 143–7
——, "James Joyce and James Stephens: The Record of a Friendship with Unpublished Letters from Joyce to Stephens," *James Joyce Quarterly*, 11 (Spring 1974) 279–92
——, "Literature and Nationality in the Work of James Stephens," *South Atlantic Bulletin*, 40 (Nov 1975) 18–25
——, "The Sources of James Stephens's *Reincarnations*: 'Alone I Did It, Barring for the Noble Assistance of the Gods,'" *Tulane Studies in English*, 22 (1977) 143–53.
——, and Patricia McFate (eds.), *Journal of Irish Literature*, A James Stephens Number, 4 (Sep 1975)
Friedman, Barton R, "Returning to Ireland's Fountains: Nationalism and James Stephens," *Arizona Quarterly*, 22 (Autumn 1966) 232–52
——, "William Blake to James Stephens: The Crooked Road," *Éire-Ireland*, 1 (Fall 1966) 29–57

Gogarty, Oliver St. John, "James Stephens," *Colby Library Quarterly*, Ser. 5 (Mar 1961) 205–15

Gordon, John D., "A Doctor's Benefaction: The Berg Collection at the New York Public Library," *Papers of the Bibliographical Society of America*, 48 (4th quart. 1954) 303–14

Gwynn, Stephen L., *Irish Books and Irish People* (London: T. F. Unwin, 1919)

——, *Irish Literature and Drama in the English Language: A Short History* (London: T. Nelson & Sons, 1936)

Hatvary, George Evon, "Re-reading 'The Crock of Gold,' " *Irish Writing*, No. 22 (Mar 1953) 57–65

Hoare, Dorothy, *The Works of Morris and Yeats in Relation to Early Saga Literature* (Cambridge: Cambridge University Press, 1937)

Hoult, Norah, "James Stephens," *Irish Writing*, No. 27 (June 1954) pp. 54–8

Joyce, James, *Letters of James Joyce*, Vol. 1, ed. Stuart Gilbert (New York: Viking, 1957); Vols. 2 and 3, ed. Richard Ellmann (New York: Viking, 1966)

Kelly, Blanche Mary, *The Voice of the Irish* (New York: Sheed & Ward, 1952)

Kiely, Benedict, *Modern Irish Fiction. A Critique* (Dublin: Golden Eagle Books, 1950)

Marcus, David, "One Afternoon with James Stephens," *Irish Writing*, No. 14 (March 1951) pp. 43–7

Marshall, H. P., "James Stephens," *London Mercury*, 12 (Sep 1925) 500–10

McFate, Patricia Ann, "*Deirdre* and 'The Wooing of Becfola,' " in *Toward the Modern: Portents of the "Movement," 1880–1920* (Carbondale: Southern Illinois University Press, 1972) pp. 165–71

——, "James Stephens' *Deirdre* and Its Legendary Sources," *Éire-Ireland*, 4 (Autumn 1969) 87–93

——, "James Stephens' Verso Additions to the Manuscripts of *The Crock of Gold*," *Bulletin of the New York Public Library*, 73 (May 1969) 328–44

Mercier, Vivian, "James Stephens: His Version of Pastoral," *Irish Writing*, No. 14 (March 1951) pp. 48–57

Morris, Lloyd R., *The Celtic Dawn: A Survey of the Renascence in Ireland, 1889–1916* (New York: Macmillan, 1917)

Pyle, Hilary, *James Stephens: His Works and an Account of His Life* (London: Routledge & Kegan Paul, 1965)

Roberts, Edward, "An Evening with James Stephens," *Dalhousie Review*, 32 (Spring 1952) 54–5

Rothenstein, William, *Since Fifty: Men and Memories, 1922–1938* (New York: Macmillan, 1940)

Russell, George, *Letters from A.E.*, ed. Alan Denson (London, New York and Toronto: Abelard-Schuman, 1961)

Saul, George Brandon, *Stephens, Yeats, and Other Irish Concerns* (New York: New York Public Library, 1954)

——, "Withdrawn in Gold," *Arizona Quarterly*, 9 (Summer 1953) 115–31

Shafer, Robert, "James Stephens and the Poetry of the Day," *Forum*, 50 (Oct 1913) 560–9

Short, Clarice, "James Stephens' Women," *Western Humanities Review*, 10 (Summer 1956) 285–8

Weygandt, Cornelius, *The Time of Yeats* (New York: D. Appleton-Century, 1937)

Yeats, W. B., *The Letters of W. B. Yeats*, ed. Allan Wade (London: R. Hart-Davis, 1954)

Index of Works by James Stephens

176   Index of Works by James Stephens

General Index